Trish –
You

Good Riddance
SHOWING CLUTTER THE DOOR

BY

SUSAN BORAX

AND

HEATHER KNITTEL

Good Riddance Professional

Organizing Solutions, Inc.

GOOD RIDDANCE
Professional Organizing Solutions, Inc.

21-3980 Canada Way
Burnaby, BC V5G 1G7
www.goodriddance.ca

Copyright © 2010 by Susan Borax
Copyright © 2010 by Heather Knittel
Cover Design & Layout: George Triay Design

Library and Archives Canada Cataloguing in Publication

Borax, Susan, 1948-
    Good riddance : showing clutter the door / Susan
Borax and Heather Knittel.

ISBN 978-0-9867177-0-3

1. House cleaning. 2. Storage in the home.
3. Orderliness. I. Knittel, Heather, 1955- II. Title.

TX324.B67 2010   648   C2010-905835-6

Printed in Canada

Praise For Good Riddance

"In my fantasy world my dream job would be that of a professional organizer. So that said, I was eager to check out Susan and Heather's book. From cover-to-cover, *Good Riddance: Showing Clutter the Door* is a well-organized (no surprise, right?) entertaining guide that doesn't lecture, but rather motivates the reader to stand up and conquer clutter. In fact it inspired me to take another look around my house for what the authors call CRUD (Completely Ridiculous Useless Debris). I am happy to report that I have said goodbye to a handful of soy sauce packets, a dozen sets of take-out chopsticks and a large stack of old home design magazines. And you know what? It felt great."

Dana Gee
Contributor, Global TV
Columnist, The Province

" This book is right on. It's gets straight to the point, room by room, and is light-hearted and funny. I laughed out loud. I really liked the afterword, where Susan and Heather encourage women to stop over-scheduling and over-reaching in order to stay on the de-cluttered path. Women need to take the time to nurture their homes as well as themselves."

Suzanne White
Home Organizer

PRAISE FOR GOOD RIDDANCE

"I need this book! Last night we started cleaning out a storage room and the biggest problem we had was releasing the feelings one has for all the stuff we've collected. I feel hostage to things from our families that are hard to part with. Guess we all do."

Barbara Teasley
Retired teacher

"The text reads very quickly and smoothly, as it should for this type of book, and the humor keeps it animated. I am definitely inspired on a few clutter issues!"

Joyce Statton
Writer/editor

"Susan Borax and Heather Knittel are two efficient and dynamic ladies who deliver an excellent de-cluttering service. They have been an invaluable resource to my clients who have prospered selling their homes after using their services. You bring more money to the table every time you get rid of stuff and Good Riddance helps you do that!"

Nargis Kakar, realtor
Sutton Group, Coquitlam

Praise For Good Riddance

"I've had the utmost pleasure working with Susan and Heather. My real estate clients are awestruck by their work and the fun they have in the process. These inspiring women teach new life skills that keep customers coming back for more.

Their fun-loving personalities come through page after page. *Good Riddance* is a quick, enjoyable read – light-hearted and funny. But be careful – you just might get an unstoppable urge to purge."

Helen Grant, realtor
Remax Crest North Vancouver

"Susan's help was priceless. She held my hand and guided me through a very difficult period of my life and my Dad's and helped us literally to move on."

Rita Solkin

"I am writing this on the surface of my desk which has been unearthed, thanks to Susan and Heather. The most important thing they have done is give me hope that clutter doesn't have to overtake my life and that facing it is not as scary as I thought."

Sybil Faigin
Teacher

ACKNOWLEDGMENTS

Were it not for the urgings of our former business coach Christopher V. Flett, author of *What Men Don't Tell Women About Business*, this book would still be a vague idea in our minds. At his insistence, we attended his workshop on how to secure a book deal. This was the pivotal moment when our spark became a flame.

There would certainly be no book if our wonderful, clutter-challenged clients had not been willing to share their stories, memories, fears and humanity with us. We are grateful for their candor, humor and generosity. How else could we have come to understand that everyone saves the same junk?

Special appreciation goes to our friends, business associates, colleagues and cherished family members who have supported and encouraged us through the growth of our business and the creation of this volume. Linda Doherty and Joan Conklin proved invaluable as early readers and critics. Our partners, Kim Yarnold and Brenda Kay, fellow cast members in our musical revue *Cluttermania* helped us appreciate that people's relationships with their clutter can be highly entertaining.

Special thanks to our editor Johanne Leach who after reading our draft manuscript while vacationing in Arizona, was so inspired she de-cluttered her condo before returning home. Our book designer George Triay never ceases to amaze us with his

ACKNOWLEDGMENTS

creativity. Special kudos to our trusted and creative photographer Claudette Carracedo whose talent with a camera is unsurpassed. We owe a debt of gratitude to graphic designer Debbie Bowles whose brilliant Good Riddance logo demonstrated how a six-inch, high-heeled shoe can be put to good use.

Susan Borax
Heather Knittel

Co-founders
Good Riddance Professional Organizing Solutions, Inc.
Burnaby, BC

Good Riddance

SHOWING CLUTTER THE DOOR

BY

SUSAN BORAX

AND

HEATHER KNITTEL

—— TABLE OF CONTENTS ——

CHAPTER 1

WHAT WE'D LEAVE IN THE FIRE

In the middle of the night, your home catches fire. You have only moments to escape. Your adrenalin is pumping. Close your eyes and visualize what would make you happy if it burned. Indulge your fantasies. What makes you cringe? Does the offending item belong to someone else in the household? Did it come from a dead relative you couldn't abide when she was alive? Has it been there since the Lusitania sank? Is it gooey, smelly or cobweb-infested?

Imagine how cathartic it would be to witness your husband's entire super-heroes comic book collection stored in the garage go up in flames. You could park the car. Envision that mountain of old textbooks reduced to a pile of ashes. Picture all the old crayon stubs, dead batteries, unread mail, the shattered fish tank and boom boxes the size of tractor-trailers vaporized. Dare to dream of a life minus the burden of CRUD: Completely Ridiculous Useless Debris.

The concept of life without CRUD tempts us all. Joan is a single woman living in the home where she raised three children. Retired and currently at a crossroads in her life, she contemplates downsizing to a condo while still in good health. Yet the idea of dealing with her possessions overwhelms her. Joan is a member of the juggernaut Baby Boomer generation. Joan's mother and father, products of the Great Depression and the Second World War, suffered deprivation in their childhood; as a result they gave their daughter everything, creating a conspicuous consumer in embryo. Today Joan not only owns her own bountiful collection of furniture, art, electronics, tools, dinnerware, etc. but she's also inherited what her parents left behind. Additionally, Joan stores her adult children's memorabilia. In other words, she has it all.

As professional organizers, we've learned that, like Joan, for most of us the struggle to keep clutter under control has less to do with pathological underpinnings than the ordinary demands of living. While many people err on the keep-too-much side, they are hardly in danger of being evicted or discovered dead beneath mountains of their own personal debris.

What is remarkable is that although our clients come to us under vastly different circumstances, they have similar collections. Some have lived in homes for 30 years or more, finding they must move to retirement communities or small condos. Others are busy people with families and hectic schedules. Somewhere along the line they have neglected to take stock of what they own. Other people have been dealt serious blows with their physical, emotional or mental health. Many prospective clients contact us on behalf of people they live with because junk is causing conflict in their relationships.

Whatever their situation, our clients are tethered to an

almost identical list of possessions. We have spent more than five years toiling side-by-side with people who require comfort while disposing of unopened but expired vitamins. We've endured paper cuts and dried out cuticles sorting through acres of paperwork. We've driven thousands of miles to recycling depots with broken appliances and we've donated enough office supplies to outfit a contingent of accounting professionals.

We routinely encounter the identical 101 household clutter items responsible for congestion in our homes. That is what this book is about. What are they? Where are they? What do you do with them? These are the 101 you hope Godzilla will obliterate by stepping through your roof on his way to crushing a packed movie theater. It's the stuff you ignore, forget, hide, pile up or lose. Rigor mortis sets in each time you get close to tackling it, like examining one of those boxes from three moves ago. You tell yourself the kids will go through it when you die. But you are only 41. As our name suggests and our mantra advocates – Good Riddance to Bad Rubbish. Before you can get organized, you need to reduce.

This book will not concentrate on alphabetizing your spices, color-coding your files or hanging your wardrobe to resemble a full-spectrum rainbow. We will reveal what's holding your house and your peace of mind hostage. Think of *Good Riddance: Showing Clutter the Door* as tough love for your least valued possessions.

Chances are you've experienced a few failed attempts at reducing clutter. Perhaps you took a half-hearted stab at the entranceway to clear up the shoes, clothes, mitts, backpacks and flyers.

You may be an empty nester who would like to transform an adult child's former bedroom into a craft studio. The adolescent furniture is in there still, but now it has company like old window fans made obsolete by central air. You might have enlisted the help of a neat-freak friend whose own house emits the aura of a display suite. That didn't work for you. The stuff you bagged up for donation is in the garage, waiting for you to call for a charity pickup.

Success in taming clutter is dependent on commitment. Nobody can make you do it. You must reach the conclusion to de-clutter for your own sake, not to appease family, friends or co-workers. We can provide you with a rationale and a framework by which to approach a task so onerous it has tested the stability of marriages, induced nausea and driven people to drink.

If a three-alarm blaze is not your idea of a workable solution, we invite you to join us on a systematic search and destroy mission that identifies these 101 offenders and why they have to go. Once these worthless items are removed, clutter will cease to cause chronic dissatisfaction with your living space. Once you have emptied your home of the marginal and unwanted, maintaining your space will be relatively simple.

CRUD IDENTIFIERS

- Something that seemed important but now is laughable, such as an award for perfect attendance at school or a Cub Scout badge for carving a wooden car.

- Anything that needs to be assembled but never was.

- Any project you started but never completed, such as baby booties for your daughter who received her MBA this year.

- Gadgets that don't work and require batteries to operate.

- Gifts you bought but neglected to give.

- Presents you received but wouldn't be caught dead wearing or displaying in your home.

- Impulse purchases bought on the shopping channel during a bout of depression that you've never shown to anyone.

- Any box you are afraid to open

- Items that require hand-washing, ironing, refinishing or reupholstering.

- Doilies.

CHAPTER 2

I JUST NEED TO GO THROUGH IT

The hardest part is getting started. While dead easy for some, throwing things away is counter-intuitive for others. The reluctant disposers withstand intolerable living conditions for years. Then something changes. They have babies, lose their jobs, get sick, or take a vacation. Stuck at home for the duration, they take a close look at their living quarters and ponder, "How did I accumulate so much stuff?" As they look around, the true implications sink in. "What was I thinking? Why is that still here?"

We have been treated to every excuse for avoiding de-cluttering, from the classic "I may need that some day" to "I just need to go through it." Our clients have hidden belongings in their cars to avoid persecution from family members. Other clients continue to rent storage lockers year after year rather than surrender a single treasure.

We've seen too many attempts gone awry. Consequently, we've developed our own Ten Commandments. Violating any single one can bring the whole operation to a halt.

1. NEVER UTTER THE "F" WORD

The root of all evil, the words "for now" are responsible for the lion's share of clutter in every home. Who has not trespassed? "I will deal with this later. I will just put it here 'for now.'" The phone rings. You're juggling packages and mail. The doorbell chimes. Whatever form the distraction takes, the consequences are always identical. "For now" becomes forever.

What happens to your stuff when it arrives home? Do purchases remain in the car? Do they make it out of the entranceway to other rooms in the house? Do things go back to a permanent location after you've used them?

Don't fall victim to procrastination. Take the extra 20 seconds to hang the key on the key ring.

2. DON'T BE A BAG LADY WITH A HOUSE

This commandment applies to tech junkies, thrift store mavens, inveterate bargain hunters, foodies and anyone who really likes clothes. The thrill is in the purchase. Your items come home, wind up on the floor of the closet in the plastic bag, accompanied by a receipt, never to be examined again. This kind of behavior costs big time. You are always buying the same stuff over and over (scotch tape, toilet bowl cleaner) because much of what you buy is still unopened in its original bag. You also run out of space much faster, due to duplication. Don't leave your new purchases in the bags. Open them, put them away and recycle the bags.

3. DON'T OPEN MULTIPLE FRONTS

If you work in multiple rooms simultaneously, you will feel as if nothing gets accomplished. Concentrate on one room only. Every room may be begging for attention, but do not succumb. Our personal preference is to begin with the storage areas. They need to be cleared to find room for excess items removed from living areas. Resign yourself to the one-room-at-a-time rule, or risk being overwhelmed.

4. DON'T ATTEMPT TO DE-CLUTTER ANYONE ELSE

This book is for you and you only. The only stuff you can deal with is your own. We need to make that clear from the get-go. You can suggest, recommend or even lead by example, but unless your mother, daughter or boyfriend is ready, touching another person's stuff is a futile exercise that breeds conflict and resentment. Stick to your own stuff. We mean it.

5. DON'T TRY TO DO THIS ALONE

This is what can happen if you attempt to fly solo tackling a lifetime's worth of clutter. Either complete paralysis sets in, due to the magnitude of the task, or you get lost in the memories. If you can afford it, engage professional help. If finances dictate otherwise, prevail upon a trusted friend or family member not easily intimidated, someone who will ask the questions about your belongings you are afraid to ask yourself.

6. DON'T STRIVE FOR PERFECTION

Do you buy lots of those magazines with images of gracious living? Do you fantasize living in those ethereal, minimalist all-white spaces? Inspirational! However, nobody actually lives with that little stuff. So, don't be ensnared by what ultra-stylish gurus and icons achieve. They have the resources to bury the bodies elsewhere. Honesty with one's self is essential. Set realistic objectives.

7. DON'T UNDERESTIMATE HOW MUCH TIME IT TAKES

Clutter doesn't happen overnight. Why expect it to disappear in a matter of hours? You're in for the long haul. Those who've lived in places for a long time generally have more work to do. Schedule multiple appointments with yourself. Sorting will take the longest. We recommend beginning six months to a year in advance of moving – time to save yourself from bad decisions, or worse, moving things that won't fit the new décor, layout or lifestyle.

8. DON'T THROW MONEY AT IT

Resist the temptation to take all the discards and bury them in a self-storage locker as a temporary measure until you decide what to do with them. Your credit card will absorb the shockwaves caused by indecision. Use a storage facility temporarily to house excess furniture or artwork while you're renovating or staging a home for sale. Do not keep unwanted belongings in limbo for decades. Unlike the banks deemed too big to fail, the Feds won't offer bailout money for your storage expenses.

9. DON'T MAKE IT HARDER
THAN IT HAS TO BE

Whether you choose to sell, donate, or toss, select a method that causes the least wear and tear on you. Keep your sorting categories to a minimum. Going through this process is an exhausting activity, performed best in stages. Use the Internet to find resources for distribution of unusual objects or substances. Garage sales can be effective, but they require a great deal of planning, pricing and a fall-back plan for those items that don't sell. Connect with charities that will pick up your clothing and household goods. The same for auctioneers or consignment. Give your friends and family firm deadlines for taking the stuff you've saved for them.

10. DON'T LEAVE HOME EMPTY-HANDED

Once you've determined what needs to go, follow through on the exit strategy. When does the recycling truck come to your area? Make sure those bags of mixed paper and shredding are out there. Call the charities. Find out when they're in your neighborhood and plan your de-cluttering around their schedule. Don't leave bags and boxes parked in your hallway or garage for indefinite periods, as you might be tempted to review them. Be as diligent about disposal as you are with sorting.

" I'm keeping that bench seat from my old mini van so I can store my complete set of Hardy Boys mysteries off the garage floor. "

CRUD logic from a man holding on to a seat from his long-gone vehicle.

CHAPTER 3

TIMING IS EVERYTHING

Procrastination is the common denominator among the clutter-challenged. If you are like our clients, you most likely require some form of external motivation. Transitions often furnish inspiration.

1. Company Time

We know of no single stimulus more effective than inviting people over. Company falls into the "major fear factor" category. No matter how messy you are in private, you don't want anyone else to know about it. We recommend harnessing this discomfort to galvanize yourself into action.

2. Moving Time

What can you do with gobs of old stuff you don't want to inflict on the new space? If you deal with it before you go, you will dramatically reduce the cost of your move, while eliminating a huge source of aggravation.

3. Selling Time

If you don't do something about the junk, inside and outside of your house, your realtor will tell you to get busy. A messy, cramped appearance undermines price. You already know this if you've watched staging shows on home makeover channels. Your buyer doesn't want to think she's mistakenly entered a thrift store instead of her future residence.

4. Re-purposing Time

Each life stage has its corresponding possessions. When children grow up and move out, their former spaces present new opportunities. Not only could you rent out your daughter's room to an international student, but you could seize the opportunity to chuck out her doll collections, tank tops and unframed posters.

5. Disaster Time

The worst has happened. You've suffered water damage to the basement when the washing machine or the sewers backed up. The restorers picked up, cleaned, stored and returned your soggy merchandise. This is a brilliant occasion to re-evaluate whether you really want to have it all back. Did you miss any of it in the eight months you lived in the motel?

6. Seasonal Time

Not every assault on household clutter needs to be precipitated by a major life change. A switch in seasons requires clothing and household articles to exchange positions. Blankets are retrieved from under the bed to replace last summer's beachwear. Learn to embrace the shift of seasons as an opportunity to cull and purge.

CHAPTER 4

DISAPPEARING ACT

You are ready to begin your "search and destroy" mission. Remember, good things will happen. Prepare yourself to stumble across items like missing engagement rings, uncashed checks and other memorabilia that vanished years ago. We've unearthed missing passports, hidden jewelry and other valuables among rusted cans of cat food and other debris. These finds alone can make the entire process worth doing.

You will need some basic supplies, most of which are free or inexpensive. The five most important items are:

- garbage bags
- boxes
- tape gun
- marking pens
- labels

If you have storage bins, laundry baskets, hampers, big buckets or other household containers, we recommend you re-purpose these for the sorting process. Remember your objective is to separate the wheat from the chaff. You are not addressing permanent storage at this stage, but sorting and purging in order to get your home life into something manageable.

De-cluttering can be both physically and emotionally exhausting. Here are some tips:

› Break your work periods into chunks of three or four hours at a time, building in rest periods and nutritional breaks.

› Begin anywhere. The order is not important. Some of our clients prefer to begin in the rooms and storage areas they are not using. They find it easier to eliminate items they have not dealt with for a long time. It depends entirely on what your goal is. Do you want to re-purpose a room? Do you need to clear the whole place to put it on the market? Have you developed new interests that require space that has heretofore been designated as storage?

› Minimize the number of trips between rooms by depositing items that need moving in a box or bag that you label "Move to Another Room." You don't want to go out like a Roman candle after a half hour's worth of sorting.

› Designate time to work on this project when your vitality is at its peak. Are you a morning person or a night owl?

" I know that plate has a huge chip and four-inch crack, but it belongs to the china set my Mom and Dad bought when they were very poor. "

CRUD logic for keeping old china.

CHAPTER 5

ENTER AT YOUR OWN RISK
A PORTAL OF THINGS TO COME

Pity the poor vestibule. It is asked to do so much, with so little real estate, serving as a launch pad for all activities conducted outside the home, as well as distribution center for all things that enter. It is also a major storage zone.

The entrance hall provides storage for raingear, boots, gloves, scarves and mittens. It's home to the trappings of animals, including leashes, balls and poop pickup bags. Most people park their keys and footwear here, too, as many North Americans have adopted the practice of removing street shoes when they enter the home.

Also found occupying the entranceway: overdue library books, serving implements or other paraphernalia that need returning. If there is a table or bench, it's likely to be littered with pairs of sunglasses, lip balm and receipts.

This is a catch-all zone that can erupt in less time than it takes a teenager to text his friends. The entranceway also happens to be the introduction to your home. Take a cold, hard look at yours. How many more quilted ski-jackets will it take before the sliding door on the hall closet derails? Would a few more strategically placed hooks allow you to unload that gargantuan hat rack?

› Umbrella's Last Stand

Warning! You are about to enter extremely dangerous territory. Tiptoe over to your coat closet and gingerly coax the door open, an inch at a time. A powerful tug could unleash a calamity – stacked-up umbrellas falling every which way, resembling a game of 52 pickup. Unchecked umbrella infestation can overtake the square footage of your hall closet in a shorter period than it would take your toddler to lose a mitten.

Did you ever wonder how they all got there? Umbrellas wind up in your possession in a myriad of ways – as a give-away at a golf tournament, the emergency purchase made during a downpour, or a gift.

The single greatest source of umbrella swarm? It's the item most left behind by guests, especially if the sun is shining when they leave.

» CRUD Challenge

You have to pare down to what a typical umbrella stand is designed to comfortably hold and no more. Start with any that have blown inside out during a sudden gust, leaving you drenched and irritated. Move on to any with defective automatic open and close options. Nothing feels quite as threatening as holding up a line of hostile passengers waiting to get on a bus during a deluge because your umbrella refuses to retract. Best alternative: move to the sunbelt and donate your umbrellas to the people doomed to live in the Pacific Northwest.

› Mail Call

Almost all organizationally challenged folks have issues around mail. Mail comes in like a trickle building up over time. If you are not vigilant, it morphs into teetering piles. Eventually that small table in your entranceway hosts a small mountain of envelopes, colorful flyers, solicitations from dryer vent cleaners and plastic-wrapped product samples of inedible breakfast snacks.

The sight of this unexamined correspondence provokes anxiety. With good reason! What's there could hurt you. How many of those envelopes contain overdue bills or insurance renewal reminders? How many harbor rejection letters from potential employers or literary agents? Are there invitations that you never responded to? And what about that fortune invested in magazines that remain unread?

» CRUD Challenge

This is a two-way challenge. Ask your utilities and other creditors to send your statements on-line. Put a sign on your front door or mailbox that says you will not accept junk mail. Consider canceling catalog subscriptions.

What about the rest of the daily torrent? Our advice is to handle paper only once. Place a recycling container where you open the mail. The envelopes, bill stuffers and ad mail will disappear like magic. Don't overcomplicate the process. Sort the contents into those needing immediate action – paying, ordering, renewing, filing, confirming – and those items that can be postponed (things you might want to read when you have the time.) Store them where you are likely to perform those activities, whether office or kitchen.

Oh yes, outgoing mail. Try taping the letter to your front door so it becomes the last thing you see on your way out. If that doesn't work, convert your bill paying to Internet banking.

› White Shoe Brigade

The athletic footwear industry has achieved worldwide hegemony rivaling only the supremacy of sunscreen manufacturers. Athletic shoes not only cost what an entire bridal ensemble would have fetched a half century ago, but there are versions engineered for every sporting activity. Multiply the number of pairs of runners by the number of household members. Did someone say tripping hazard? That pile is what you need to navigate every time you enter or leave your home. What would extra-terrestrials think if they chose your hallway to land their spacecraft? They would likely conclude that Earth was inhabited by the human equivalent of centipedes.

» CRUD Challenge

Time to get down and dirty. Match them up in pairs. Don't

expect 100 per cent success. Some are bound to be missing, left behind at a sleepover or skating rink. Separate the ones that fit from those that are outgrown. From the remaining stock eliminate any whose odor repels the family dog. If you have the space, designate a shelf or basket for each family member's currently wearable footwear. Sneakers in good condition are always candidates for donation. Listen to the Beatles' Rubber Soul album for courage.

› Captive

For many men there seems no end to the appeal of baseball caps. In the homes of our clients, caps represent every sports team ever played on, every destination and attraction ever visited and every trade show, convention or golf tournament ever attended.

They present major storage problems. Expect a landslide from the upper shelf of the coat closet or a mess on the floor if you try hanging them on hooks. In our opinion, there's only one legitimate use for baseball caps – covering up a bad hair day.

» CRUD Challenge

Open a large lawn and leaf plastic garbage bag and round them up. Primary targets are the sweat-stained and filthy. Implement a one-in one-out program to prevent further stockpiling.

CHAPTER 6

KITCHEN COUNTER OFFENSIVE
THE UNMENTIONABLE TRUTH
ABOUT YOUR CUPBOARDS

If there's a room crying out for a rescue mission, the kitchen takes top honors – the sacred burial ground for unappreciated hostess gifts and obsolete gadgets.

Kitchens keep much of the mess behind closed doors, creating the illusion of order. But open those cabinets and discover cross-pollination or, simply put, unrelated items mixed together. Over time there are no distinctions between food and non-food, tableware and cookware or utensils and paper goods. It can take more time to look for a single ingredient like sage, than to cook an 18-pound turkey. If the state of your kitchen is cause for indigestion, we recommend beginning in this heart of the house. If the going gets too tough, a bag of chips won't be too far away.

› Mug Shots

Where would most of us be without our coffee? We are the first to admit the importance of this precious liquid for our productivity, not to mention regularity. Yet what is the appropriate number of coffee cups you need to own at one time? In kitchen after kitchen, we see legions of coffee mugs hanging from curly metal trees, suspended from under the counter hooks or lined up in formation in our clients' cabinets. Some folks consider them to be collectables, hoarding cartons of them in storage.

In all probability, you won't find any two that match.

» CRUD Challenge

If you have an entire cupboard devoted to mugs, you have work to do. The first cut includes any that are chipped, cracked or have a smiley face. If you have a pellet gun, you can use these mugs for target practice. Then toss the faded ones, ones bearing the name or logo of your insurance broker and the lopsided mug crafted by your best friend in ceramic class. Tell her it broke. She'll never know. Keep your favorites. Pack the decent ones for donation, put them in your car and drop them off at a local thrift shop before nightfall.

› Frigid Dare

Can you name a home design publication that has featured a designer kitchen with a fridge magnet on any of its gleaming surfaces? Just because your refrigerator door is made of metal, does not give you the right to plaster it with a multitude of assorted fridge magnets. Talk about a blight on the interior landscape. As far as we are concerned, fridge magnets are as welcome as an invasion of roaches.

They find their way in as colorful plastic letters, clever sayings or a miniature replica of a favorite cartoon character. Semi-useful magnets contain phone numbers for emergency services or the local pizza joint. We wonder, though, if your refrigerator would be the first place you'd look if you were panicking over an overflowing toilet.

Unfortunately, the magnet collection pegs you somewhat short of the edgy, trend-spotting, style-conscious decorator you may think you are.

» CRUD Challenge

How do you know when to quit? When you can't find the door handle? If you must keep a few, limit yourself to a small number of worthy examples. If it were up to us, we'd recommend keeping the ones that say: "Make yourself at home. Clean my kitchen." Or fridge magnets that threaten retribution for eating the last piece of cheesecake.

› The Ten Condiments

No Chinese take-out meal would seem complete without the requisite assortment of sauces and fortune cookies, right? Yet loading up on freebies is antithetical to maintaining an organized home.

Leftover miniature sauce packages frolic in the drawer with renegade toothpicks, old bottle caps, straws, drink umbrellas and a couple of paper napkins. Over time, you can accumulate quite a stash. Around the time that you are no longer able to close the drawer, mull over the idea of thinning out the collection.

» CRUD Challenge

Thou shalt not save any of the following:

1. Soy sauce packets
2. Sweet and sour sauce packets
3. Artificial sweeteners from the coffee shop
4. Tartar sauce packets
5. Tiny coffee creamers
6. Mustard packages
7. Mayo packages
8. Salt and pepper shakers from airplanes
9. Wasabi packets
10. Crackers that come with soup

› No Can Do

Canned food does not last forever. There is a shelf life to every can. We prefer the term the British use – the death date. As professional organizers, we have witnessed more than our share of unspeakable cupboard disasters, the result of cans left too long on the shelf. Sometimes they explode, leaving a residue like asphalt. Other times they spring leaks and cement themselves to the cabinet. The most vulnerable include pineapple and tomato-based products.

Old canned food can be found in the same Bermuda Triangle where broken toasters, juicers bought on the home shopping channel and ice cube trays from the old refrigerator reside. We refer here to the lower corner cabinet, a cavern so deep that even household pets have been known to disappear.

» CRUD Challenge

Do not for a second think about giving that expired food to the food bank. Take an hour or so to comb through the cans. Dented ones go first, then anything with a coating of dust. If you can't read the "best before" date and can't remember where, when or why you bought the chickpeas, err on the side of caution. It's your life.

› Polygamy

The ubiquitous plastic bag, an environmental pariah, is a blight on the landscape. Although retail outlets are replacing them with re-usable cloth alternatives, wherever we go we find hundreds under bathroom and kitchen sinks, in broom closets and wardrobes. We had one client who lived in a 350-square-foot apartment who stockpiled them for the day he got a dog. His landlord did not allow pets.

Save a few for legitimate uses like preventing your

hair gel from oozing in your suitcase in flight or lining a wastepaper basket.

» CRUD Challenge

When you're purging your collectables and bric-a-brac, wrap the fragile and breakable items in the plastic bags. Your junk will arrive at its ultimate destination unharmed and you will be bag-free in no time. Otherwise, invest in a dog.

› Plastic Surgery

Leftovers never had it so good. Plastic containers come in an infinite variety of shapes and sizes. You can buy them by the carload in big box stores. If this isn't enough, they enter your home like inverted Trojan horses disguised as yogurt, potato salad and deli containers. Collectively, they can garner more kitchen cabinet and refrigerator space than your pots and pans, glassware and everyday dishes combined.

Why, you ask? They fall into that netherworld category described as "too good to throw out." People feel they have a sacred obligation to save them, regardless of how space-challenged they are. When there are too many, the excess hides in the pantry, linen closet or guest room. But it's not just the sheer order of magnitude that's the predicament: if you were to eyeball your own supply of plastic ware, we would wager that 40 percent is missing either lids or bottoms.

» CRUD Challenge

That blue plastic bin collecting spider webs in your garage is called a recycling bin. It's designed specifically for plastic, cans and glass. Use it. Be realistic about the quantity and variety of containers you actually rely on for lunches, storing non-food items, etc. and relieve your cramped cabinets of the overkill.

› The Weight of Water

Could you imagine going to the gym without a water bottle? Reusable bottles, both of the plastic and metal variety are the choice of millions. Water bottles supply refreshment minus the trip to the dreaded public water fountains. Whether it's a heightened paranoia about germs or vivid elementary school flashbacks of abandoned wads of someone else's chewing gum inches from your lips, personal water vessels are the clear preference over the public offering.

And why not? You get one for every team sport you participate in or every marathon you run. Water bottles come with gym memberships. Kitchen cupboards become the main repository for retired and semi-retired bottles. Even when they have leaky or missing caps, water bottles are retained for nostalgic reasons.

» CRUD Challenge

Donation or recycling is our best suggestion here. After

disposal, go out and buy yourself a decent set of martini glasses. You will need them to get through the other 101 items on the list.

› You Should Cook So Long

We direct the foodie to listen up. Cease and desist your recipe clipping compulsion. How many ways can you cook a chicken? For those of you who suffer from the bulging drawer and/or dog-eared binder of food-stained family favorites, or worse yet, harbor them on index cards in a green plastic box, we have a news flash. Even if you quit your day job, swallowed a box of caffeine pills and cooked three gourmet meals a day, every day, for the next 20 years, no way could you get through a third of the recipes you've been stockpiling. And remember, you can find any recipe you need on the Internet, even the ones you clipped from magazines.

*" My cat likes the height of that cat tree.
When she looks out the window she is
exactly in line with the cherry tree
the birds land in all the time. "*

*CRUD logic from a woman explaining a
split-level cat tree in her living room.*

» CRUD Challenge

Where to begin? How about the pineapple upside down cake recipe when you're struggling with that spare tire around your middle? Clear out the loose magazine clippings from supermarket giveaway publications and any recipe that uses cream of chicken soup as the main ingredient. Consider canceling subscriptions to those fancy gourmet magazines – we think of them as food porn. Don't replace the contents of the recipe drawer with take-out menus. You can get them online, too.

› Rack Attack

Herbs and spices provide zing to home-cooked meals. Spice racks, readily available in an unlimited variety of styles and finishes to complement almost any kitchen décor, offer that one-stop approach for meal preparation. They make great shower and housewarming gifts and are the very model of organization with their labels and their own mini shelves.

Although initially they look good and make you feel like a chef by association, they experience a rapid decline in potency. When you contain dried spices in transparent glass jars, they become tasteless and thus useless. After a few years on your counter, spice racks develop a greasy film that makes those fancy labels illegible. Fresh herbs win hands down for pure flavor.

Spice racks become one more counter space hog like the sugar bowl or the mixer. We have carted away more old spice racks than we'd care to recall.

» CRUD Challenge

Dump out all of the lifeless seeds and leaves and recycle the glass jars. When you replace the contents, store them in an interior cabinet or drawer where they won't be destroyed by light. Re-purpose the little shelves as holding pens for mystery screws or little cheese spreaders.

› Vasectomy

Who among us does not enjoy the way a bouquet of fresh flowers perks up a room or dining table? Yet why does every receptacle that enters the home bearing floral displays become a permanent fixture? Are vases yet another example of the "too good to throw away" syndrome? Open that annoying and useless cabinet above the refrigerator where your extra vases are apt to live. Some vessels are for buds, many are clear and a few may be crystal. In our estimation, four or five should cover the range in size and variety. If your collection surpasses 15, consider a thrift store donation soon.

» CRUD Challenge

Separate the sublime from the mundane. Keep the heirlooms or wedding presents. Ditch the duplicates and any that acknowledged the birth of your baby. Donate the excess to a continuing education program teaching floral design.

› The OK Corral

We believe the ubiquitous junk drawer is a necessary evil for a simple reason. As a fundamental organizing principle, we advocate storing similar items together. But many household articles defy categorization. The junk drawer serves as a sacrificial lamb so that the rest of the drawers can maintain their orderly appearance. However, when we say a junk drawer, we do mean ONE, not one in every room. The kitchen is the best location.

What populates the average household junk drawer? We have identified our own top 20. Twist ties, plastic bread tabs, wine bottle corks and rubber bands head our list. Corks present puzzlement. Everyone knows there's no point in re-corking a bottle of champagne. It will go flat, so you might as well finish it. If you leave too many corks in your junk drawer, you risk your children thinking you belong in Alcoholics Anonymous.

As long as there's broccoli, there will be a steady supply of brightly hued, thick rubber bands to add color accents to junk drawers.

Other junk drawer tenants that we extract include expired coupons, miniature sticky note pads, toys from fast food joints, bakery box string, corn on the cob holders, key chains, uneaten Halloween candy, loose change, unidentified telephone numbers, ballpoint pens that don't write, dog biscuits, audio cassettes, flashlights and address labels sent out by charities. We are certain you have many of your own to add to the list.

» CRUD Challenge

Much of what plagues a junk drawer can be solved in minutes and for a few dollars. Dump the contents and purge the overabundance you cannot use before collecting social security. Separate what remains into logical categories, keeping office type supplies away from cat litter sifters or bus schedules.

Visit your local dollar store and purchase square and rectangular small plastic baskets in a couple of different sizes. Arrange them in the drawers and fill them with your flotsam and jetsam. The next time you open the drawer, it will glide out.

› Scorch Song

What cook has not coped with the self-loathing that results after leaving a pot on the stove too long? Each time you pick up that cooking utensil, it serves as a painful reminder of past culinary disasters like the turkey breast cutlets that became indistinguishable from hockey pucks, while you chatted long-distance to your oldest friend. Why go on reliving the mishap day after day? When we are working with our clients' kitchen cupboards, we witness myriads of blackened and rusted metal, mostly in the form of baking pans, roasting pans and cookie sheets. Baking utensils usurp 25 to 30 per cent of kitchen storage space.

» CRUD Challenge

Here is how the conversation goes with our clients when we suggest they part with a much cherished pan that has barely survived the birth of a volcano.

"Oh, I can't get rid of that. My great-aunt used it for her noodle pudding." We counter with, "Have you ever made anything in it? Do you plan to?"

If you have more space than you know what do to with, you are in the unique position of being able to hoard all the cookware you want. But, if you are desperately holding on to your sanity trying to prepare meals in a kitchen with barely enough counter space for a Magic Bullet, ditch those deteriorating pans and give yourself some breathing space.

*" If my sister who lives in Winnipeg dies
in the winter, I'll need that heavy
overcoat to wear to her funeral. "*

*CRUD logic from a husband to wife trying
to clear out their bulging hall closet.*

CHAPTER 7

DINING ROOM DISORDERS

Some dining areas host meals on a daily basis. Others are reserved only to mark special occasions, instantly recognizable by the formal chandelier hung above the middle of the table. In these cases the dining room resembles a cross between a storage locker and a museum sheltering an array of entertaining and eating implements, many received as engagement or wedding gifts. A significant number of the gifts may be in their original packaging.

If you think a charger plate is a synonym for a credit card, better spend some concentrated time de-cluttering this part of your home.

› Martha Speaks

Let's take the tarnish test. Pull out all of the silver and silver plate flatware, serving spoons, the tea service, candlesticks, chafing dishes and salt cellars from their hiding place. How dull and blackened are they? That will give you some insight into how long it has been since you've used any of this finery. If you didn't inherit these treasures you may have received them as wedding gifts from the era when brides were brainwashed to believe they needed all this stuff to set a proper table. The silver chafing dishes are the tip of the iceberg.

» CRUD Challenge

If you're holding on to the silver to pass on to the children, think again. Like many an heirloom, your kids don't want it. Silver is high maintenance, and who has time to polish the tea service when you can't find time to polish your nails? Sell it. Bring in a trustworthy antique dealer or appraiser. Find out the current market value. Then drag out the jar of polish one last time.

› Waxed Out

Candles make for lovely decorative accents, creating atmosphere or mood. A bedroom transforms into a boudoir. A bathroom becomes a Roman spa with 20 or 30 glowing cylinders.

Be honest. How many candles do you think you own? Don't forget those itty-bitty tea lights purchased by the hundreds, the tapers, pillars, Chanukahs, votive globes, the scented and the fragrance-free. Then add the accessories designed to display them: candelabras, hurricane lamps, candlesticks and hanging lanterns for the garden, to name a few. Ka-ching, Ka-ching! No wonder they are the darlings of the home party circuit. Who can resist all that warmth and beauty?

Our beef? Do not cling to the half-melted, coagulated pool of liquefied paraffin topped off with a crusty, charred wick now glued to your coffee table.

» CRUD Challenge

Start your personal operation snuff with the rim of your bathtub. Then turn your attention to the blobs adorning your bedroom. Proceed with garbage bag in hand to every corner of your abode and eradicate the offending items. Use a chisel to remove the drips. All kidding aside, if it's ambience you crave, buy a dimmer.

› Table Clothes

We bet that at least one of your dining room buffet drawers is stacked to the gunnels with hand-knitted potholders, cocktail aprons, doilies, cloth napkins, a quilted tea cozy and an endless array of tablecloths in every size and shape. Some have grease spots or wine stains. You cling to them because they came from your grandmother. Why are you saving them? You go out to eat four nights a week.

» CRUD Challenge

The low-hanging fruit lies in the one-off napkins, potholders woven to get a badge in Brownies and anything with a hole in it. Get started with these and move yourself up the chain to higher-level decision making – table runners, napkin rings and any tablecloths that require ironing.

› A Matter of Place

Second cousin to the aforementioned dreaded drawer of unused table linen is the placemat cache – summer ones for BBQs, fancy ones for holidays, singles and doubles, and, of course the omnipresent plastic selection. The plastic ones stick together from caked on food. Some are actually laminated pre-school crayon drawings executed by your budding Michelangelo at an early age. Others reprise a faded elementary school picnic photo where your own progeny is all but unrecognizable.

» CRUD Challenge

Don't get too hung up on these table protectors – there are far bigger fish to fry in this volume. With a minimal effort you can accomplish miracles. Be certain to remove the drawer completely as there are bound to be one or two crumb-laden specimens that have wedged themselves into the rear. Placemats do warrant replacement at least every ten years. Apply the one-in one-out principle to this exercise and revel in the endorphins furnished by a retail outing.

› Home Plate

Dishes are to kitchens and dining rooms what rabbits are to the animal kingdom. If you allow them, they will breed behind the closed doors of your cupboards. By the time many of our clients have reached their middle years, they are well on their way to owning four or five sets – the everyday variety and the good china for company. Lots have plastic sets for outdoor entertaining. Others collect teacups, saucers and luncheon sets. Some hold on to their mother's and sometimes grandmother's china, no matter how chipped or crackled. Dishes rank highly on the emotional attachment scale, so editing needs kid gloves.

» CRUD Challenge

If you're planning on foisting your extra sets of dishes on your children, you are making a huge miscalculation. Get more creative. The once revered china patterns, some of which require hand washing, so coveted a generation or two ago, have lost their appeal in addition to their gold leaf rims.

Unless you have full sets, in pristine condition, selling is an unlikely proposition. Donate individual pieces to thrift stores or unload them at garage sales, flea markets and swap meets. Treat yourself to the good stuff more often instead of saving it for guests.

> *" I'm holding onto this croquet set*
> *in case I ever have a lawn. "*

CRUD logic from long time resident
of a high-rise apartment.

CHAPTER 8

FRIGHT OF THE LIVING ROOM
RECLINERS & OTHER DECORATING ANATHEMAS

There are many terms to describe this most public of spaces in the home. Over the decades it has gone by many names – the salon, parlor or living room depending on the era in which one spent one's formative years. For those who grew up in the middle of the last century, the living room was forbidding in its formality – a room in which one entertained company. Otherwise, it was off limits. It might as well have been cordoned off with velvet ropes for the amount of human traffic it saw. Plastic slipcovers adorned the upholstery, warning even visitors that no one could be trusted with a burning cigarette or a glass of red wine.

A great deal of the stuffiness disappeared as the living room gave way to the family room and evolved into an active hub, no longer the preserve of adults and children seen, but not heard. Today it serves as playroom, entertainment center, makeshift dining area, homework and hobby center. Clutter thrives in chaotic environments such as these

› Control Freaks

For men, the remote control represents a modern day

security blanket, akin to a beer can. For women these handheld devices are pariahs due to the frequency with which their programs are interrupted by their male partners through frenetic channel changing.

Unlike prehistoric times when people manually changed channels, every electronic home entertainment appliance arrives with its own remote.

Not only does this add a storage problem, the new equipment presents a dilemma: which do you use for what.

Have you noticed how often remotes go missing, possibly mistaken for portable phones and deposited in other rooms? Do you want to wager that after you've upgraded to a 60-inch flat-screen, wall-mounted home theater system the old orphaned remote will still lurk in the assorted collection on your coffee table?

» CRUD Challenge

These puppies hide everywhere. A good place to look is under the cushions on the couch where they fall between the cracks. If you can't tell what a remote is for, check the manufacturer and see if you have a stereo component or DVD player with that name. Or was it sold in last year's garage sale?

› Throwbacks

Practically a pandemic, throw pillows proliferate in the

domestic landscape. Did you ever sit on a sofa overflowing with these decorative accents without disturbing their perfect symmetry? You need to balance on the outer edge of the couch, back straight.

Couches and loveseats come with their own miniature cushion duo, but that's not enough to satisfy today's slaves to home fashion trends. Floral, striped, solid, velvet, beaded and heart-shaped – you name it – some are complete with cute sayings. We would like to see one that says "Whenever I feel the urge to throw something away, I lie down until the feeling passes." Dust magnets, par excellence.

» CRUD Challenge

If you can't bear to part with them all, at least consider editing out the sun-faded, food-stained and cat-clawed specimens – and anything with fringe.

› Creature Comfort

We are not certain whether clients ever buy recliners or if they simply inherit them. Nothing dates a room more than the presence of one of these knobby plaid-upholstered behemoths, and owning one adds 20 years to your age. You can update your lighting, change your color scheme and add crown molding, but if the recliner remains you're in the heart of the 1950s. Plus, they take up a lot of space. When the footrest reaches its full extension, your recliner could be mistaken for an aircraft carrier.

» CRUD Challenge

Have you ever known anyone who remained awake after ten minutes of TV viewing in a recliner? Maybe you know an insomniac who would welcome it. If the idea of chucking the recliner wounds your decorating sensibilities, move it to the bedroom or spare room.

› Macramé

Ah, the seventies – burnt orange, fake walnut veneer furniture and the vintage stereo. Perhaps the most emblematic symbol of that forgettable decade is the macramé plant hanger. We find them anchored to the ceilings in our clients' homes by ornate brass hooks. Occasionally we even find a living, although slightly dehydrated, plant.

» CRUD Challenge

Macramé perseveres. Clients would sooner shed their lava lamps, Afro hair picks and Nehru jackets than surrender their beaded, shredded, faded and dated creations. Who are we to judge? Those days as a hippie may have been the happiest time in their lives.

We guess you are not pre-disposed to throwing these away. We get that. "They are in good condition," you plead. You insist that someone will want them if they are donated. We counter by telling you that nobody wants them. Well, almost nobody. There are those fringe people who haunt the universe of second-hand retailing who will buy absolutely anything. Don't let that be you in 30 years. The time to tackle this is now. Face it. Once the macramé disappears, you'll never give it another thought.

If you cannot bear to part with your old macramé plant hangers, here are a few suggestions:

- Attach them together to create a hammock.
- Use them in a closet to store dead tennis balls to throw for the dog.
- Use them for catching tadpoles at the lake.

› Snack Attack

We are not sure which came first, the TV dinner or the snack table. About the time North Americans dispensed with the family dinner table in favor of chowing down in front of the evening news or payola-corrupted game shows, a flimsy set of four folding tables became de rigueur. Actually they were primarily plastic trays attached to highly unstable metal legs designed for easy storage. Decorated with paintings of elks in their pristine natural settings, they provided the perfect platform for the less than gourmet fare served by grateful housewives tired of cooking night after night. When you're looking for a scapegoat to explain the demise of the traditional mealtime discourse, look no further than the humble snack table.

These tables were designed to be wiped down and returned to the pantry or corner storage after meal or snack time. Instead they have become permanent fixtures, littered with everything from candy wrappers to stacks of unopened mail, supermarket circulars and single socks. A mere nudge sends them toppling to the floor.

» CRUD Challenge

You may think these harmless, stackable furniture items are undeserving of purge consideration. After all, they hardly take up any space. If you're holding on to them for sentimental reasons – such as they are a relic from your childhood – then by all means keep them. Find a nice cozy corner in the basement. Since you already have a flat-screen wall-mounted TV in your kitchen, no need to set them up in the family room with your fiber-enhanced liquefied meal replacements when you watch *The View.*

" *When my friends from Alberta visit they like their coffee made in this.* "

CRUD logic from a woman unwilling to part with a broken percolator with missing lid.

› Black Thumb

Not everyone is lucky enough to be born with the indoor gardening gene, but a little watering goes a long way.

When the lush splendor of the healthy potted mum delivered to you in the hospital has been reduced to a spindly, brownish stalk jutting from a pot of cracked earth, consider the garbage receptacle. If your windowsill is dotted with a number of these beauties, several of them sporting insect colonies, we suggest a pet rock is more in keeping with your nurturing abilities.

Live plants are messy. They drop leaves, leak, leave water stains on tabletops and carpets, and fall over. They need fertilizing. In other words, they need devotion. Are they worth it?

» CRUD Challenge

Nothing shouts indifference like a room full of pathetic looking neglected houseplants. Watch out for the ones rooted in those adorable, special occasion baby shoe-shaped ceramic containers. Past the point of no return? Off they go. Don't for one minute consider replacing them with artificial philodendrons cascading from faux brass pots.

› Go Figure

Unless you qualify as a complete minimalist, this section applies to you.

Many names describe the ornaments embellishing mantles, coffee tables, bookshelves, end tables and window sills in today's living rooms. We refer to them as knickknacks, gewgaws, chachkas, baubles, whatnots, figurines and curios, to name a few. Commemorative plates, coins, spoons, dolls, teacups and saucers, statuettes of silent screen stars, and creamers in the shape of cows all fall into this category. Their most significant attribute? They are collectables.

Late-night TV purveyors, Internet marketers and mail order companies line up to ensure no single item fails to find its way into your china cabinet. However, when displayed in the ways we routinely observe, we recommend an earthquake.

Whether inherited, purchased on impulse or ordered from a catalog, collectables can overwhelm a room. We understand their purpose – to provide pleasure, evoke memories and express the aesthetic sensibility of the owner. We are arguing for restraint, not outright abolition.

» CRUD Challenge

Do not buy more shelving.

We tread on dangerous ground suggesting the sacrifice of the most cherished of household possessions. But think about it this way. When a realtor lists your house, he or she will banish all those trinkets for the duration of showings.

Thin out the collection now. Give some away or sell them.

Use a rotation system for the ones you keep. Consider on-line auction sites, consignment and thrift shops. Better to edit now, than the day a tight deadline looms. The good news? You won't miss the hours of dusting.

› Cat Scratch Fever

Cat lovers beware. We get all the pictures, ceramic representations and cat-shaped pillows you collect, but we can't fathom why you position those carpeted, scratching pole skyscrapers in the most prominent position in the room – the center of the picture window. Why obliterate the view with what looks like a junior high school industrial arts project gone wrong?

Sometimes we see variations in every room. The makers of cat trees and other cat gymnastic apparatus have their claws in pet owners inducing them to spend large sums to provide an indoor replica of the natural world. These four-foot, mushroom-colored feline tributes to broadloom destroy your décor. And while we are at it, what's with all the dog beds in every room? We are animal lovers ourselves. We just think that your pet shouldn't have more furniture than you do.

» CRUD Challenge

First things first. Make sure you still have a cat. If you no longer have a cat, buy that cat tree a bus ticket out of your house. If you do have a cat, put the cat tree somewhere where it will be less likely to demand attention, preferably in an area that is poorly lit. If your model is showing the ravages of age, resolve to replace it soon. The next time you are in the market for a pet, consider a cricket.

› Dried Flower Arraignment

We recommend leaving flower arranging, particularly of the dried variety, to the professionals. Yet most people insist on working with this crumbling medium at home. We have consulted in the homes of avid collectors who have kept every floral keepsake from their senior prom wrist carnations to the centerpieces from their nephew's Bar Mitzvah. These shriveled, brittle and faded floral elements wind up in every milk jug, vase and wine bottle in the house. Often woven into wreaths, they make appearances at holiday times, accompanied with the appropriate seasonal accents like gourds or pine cones. Dried flowers are of particular interest to cats who often knock them over, spreading a hailstorm of dust and powdery particles in their wake.

» CRUD Challenge

Have you ever tried to pack these fragile objects? Disintegration occurs on first contact with a piece of tissue paper. Think about the statute of limitations. When your next bouquet of fresh flowers wilts, put it out with the rest of the trash.

CHAPTER 9

BATHROOM BLIGHT
IT AIN'T JUST SOAP SCUM

Just when the number of medications, lotions, potions and apparatus per body part has reached epic proportions, the designers of bathrooms have decreased storage options.

In the 1960s, bathroom sinks came with vanities with drawer space and room for towels, extra soaps and cleansers. These have now given way to pedestal sinks.

Around the turn of the millennium, a counter-trend emerged (no pun intended). Madison Avenue convinced us we required not one, but minimally four types of sun protection, about the same time bathroom storage space went the way of the dodo bird. Big box stores reaped a bonanza in selling super-sized bottles of mouthwash and huge packages of toilet paper, while bathrooms evolved into luxury spas with steam-stall showers and no storage. Unless you are blessed with a palatial ensuite attached to your master bedroom, clutter will dominate the bathroom. You can't remove a fixture, like the toilet, so resist and reduce.

› Bathroom Humor

Do you recall the toilet tank set ensemble? The Unholy Trinity – the matching tank and toilet seat covers with their sidekick, the contour rug outlining the commode. You might still own the avocado green shag combo. We've always suspected them of being mildly unhygienic in the way sitting on a soft, cushy toilet seat can make you feel queasy. If no longer in use, the fetching threesome lies abandoned in the back of the linen closet, along with the other victims of age and neglect. We refer to the disintegrating, yellowed drawer liners, the grungy pink rubber shower mat and the Christmas hand towels (a hostess gift) trimmed in red and green.

» CRUD Challenge

Schedule these lapses in judgment for immediate departure. While you're at it, toss any hand-crocheted toilet paper covers in the shape of French poodles. Might as well make it four for four.

› Bathing Beauties

Similar to the miniature liquor bottles available on airplanes, little bottles of shampoo, conditioner, lotion and mouthwash provided by hotels exude irresistible charm even for the seasoned traveler. Add the tiny soaps, shoe mitts, sewing kits, shower caps and petite bubble baths and over time your bathroom will resemble a Lilliputian day spa. While gathering a coating of dust, they squander valuable space under the sink that could be better utilized for extra tissues. Why bother to pack them for use on your next trip when a whole new assortment will be waiting for you at you next destination?

» CRUD Challenge

If on your next hotel stay you cannot leave the tiny samples by the sink, be ruthless when you get home. Toss any old ones or any that have been partially used. Donate unopened containers to a women's shelter.

› Transparent Towels

While we are on the subject of the bathroom, check your terrycloth collection. Our clients lack the ability to part with towels no matter how threadbare.

The life cycle of the typical bath towel has several phases. It begins with enveloping you in warmth and comfort after the shower. After 50 plus washes, with fluffiness all but a distant memory, drying off with your towel is more akin to a total body exfoliation with a piece of sandpaper. This heralds the next stage: demotion to gym or beach towel status. Once the towel reaches "see-through" class, it's downgraded to wiping the dog's feet or washing the car. The final stage is that of cleaning rag. Smaller towels, like facecloths and finger towels, spiral down the hierarchy a lot faster.

» CRUD Challenge

When you see one towel in each color, you know you have

a few too many. Don't forget the old tub mats and scatter rugs, particularly the ones with the disintegrating rubber backing. Contact a local animal shelter or vet for donation.

› Good to the Last Drop

With bathroom real estate at such a premium, who can afford to litter the limited space with the dregs of old personal hygiene products? Evaluate your stash of nail polishes with the brushes imbedded in the calcified liquid. Take aim at the spray bottle disinfectant that dribbles foam instead of shooting out a steady stream of bacteria-destroying cleaning power. Who doesn't have a cosmetic case of old lipsticks whose collective contents would barely cover the surface of a pair of post-collagen treatment pillow lips? Do you really believe there is one last squeeze in that aged tube of under-eye concealer? Empty and near-empty containers squander space. Use them or lose them.

" I just need to take a picture of these. "

CRUD logic from a woman storing a record of dental impressions demonstrating the progression of her orthodontic treatments.

» CRUD Challenge

Purging the bathroom provides immediate gratification. Get rid of the extra mouthwash and dregs of dusting powder, soap slivers, eyebrow and lip pencil stubs, dried up baby and anti-bacterial wipes, sun block from five years ago and rusty tweezers.

› De-Pill-atory

In the old days, the majority of householders kept a bottle of aspirin and antacids to battle life's infirmities. Add Band-Aids, adhesive tape and a big jar of Vaseline to that meager list.

Now, by today's standards, disease doesn't stand a chance, not when pitted against the medical arsenal you've assembled to ward off unwelcome micro-organisms and promote rapid healing. We would guesstimate that the supplements, suppositories, acne cleansers, decongestants, hemorrhoid preparations, cough syrups and teeth whiteners number in the hundreds. And that doesn't cover prescription drugs.

We understand the shock of confronting your personal pharmacy. Buying medications does not qualify as impulse shopping, because when you're sick, you rarely hesitate to shop for relief. The issue lies with the transitory nature of minor maladies. That embarrassing flatulence may not repeat itself for years, but you now own a nearly full box of expired gas pills. Not only does this reservoir of expired tablets constitute a huge parking problem for your limited storage capacity, but it costs money, too. When you can't find what you need in an emergency, you run out and buy a duplicate. Instead of having one bottle of stool softeners, you now own two, likely used once a year when you travel.

Expired medications require a special protocol for safe disposal, similar to getting rid of old paint.

» CRUD Challenge

If you value your life, your money and your sanity, purge your private dispensary. Pharmacies will take your discarded prescription drugs. Recycle the plastic containers once emptied of their contents. And get rid of those ointment samples in the metal tubes with the rolled up ends and missing caps.

› Hairum Scarum

We cannot do justice to the bathroom without commenting on the H word. When was the last time you shopped for gel or shampoo in a drug store or salon? There are acres of aisles completely dedicated to hair dye, hairsprays and styling confections, all of which need storage in your bathroom. As well as the volumizers, mousses, waxes, gels and spritzes invented for the express purpose of controlling hair with a mind of its own, you very likely have another drawer or plastic container for the hardware. Curling irons, blow dryers and electric rollers hog space not to mention combs, brushes and other manual tools.

Clips, bobby pins, barrettes and scrunchies bunk in with the aforementioned hair accoutrements. And these are just the men's products!

» CRUD Challenge

Short of shaving your head, there's a solution. Start with the low-hanging fruit, meaning the really old and scary stuff, like the pink hairdryer with the oversized hood big enough to fit over your rollers. Age matters. Don't risk spraying your locks with anything that pre-dates the beehive hairdo. Scary also means nylon curler caps, ratty hairnets, plastic headbands with teeth or anything that could turn your hair green.

> *" I need that rack when the time comes for my daughters to sit shiva for me. There has to be somewhere for people to hang their coats. "*

CRUD logic for a woman declining to part with a large metal free-standing clothing rack stashed in the back of a closet.

CHAPTER 10

BEDLAM

Make your bedroom – typically reserved for sleeping, relaxation, clothing storage, grooming and romance – your sanctuary. Maintain this sector so that these activities can be enjoyed to their fullest. Be vigilant.

We often see beds laden with so much laundry, magazines, mail, newspapers and the remains of last night's dinner that sleep seems out of the question.

In the closet, we see drawers too crammed to open, shelves on the brink of collapse, unedited wardrobes sporting the same never-worn garments. Did we forget to mention shoes?

Open any night table drawer and we discover foreign coins, tangled chains, phone numbers without names, used tissues, antacid tablets and old bus passes.

The bedroom, doing double-duty as a living space and a storage area, has also become the permanent repository of miscellaneous articles unconnected to bedroom activities. In the bedroom closet we discover books, work files, classroom notes, typewriters, sporting goods, bulk food and oodles of luggage, followed by toys, dishes, unopened gifts and the occasional disintegrating vintage fur jacket. The region under the bed often houses dog-chewed shoes, maps in tubes and overflow wool from the craft room sprinkled with dust bunnies.

Most of this extraneous debris needs relocation to transform your bedroom into a personal refuge where you can escape when the clutter struggle wears you down. Trust us on this.

› Soft Shoulders

Every time we come across a bag of shoulder pads we muse about these foam rubber artifacts that defined a decade of fashion. During what other era could a woman strut around looking like a linebacker for the New York Jets and be considered chic and stylish?

Our personal theory of why shoulder pads were so popular? They were better than a diet pill. You could put on your tights, leg warmers and sweater with shoulder pads. Suddenly your rear end, paunch and thunder thighs disappeared. With shoulders as wide as a subway platform, the rest of you ceased to register. What a silhouette! Imagine a pyramid turned upside down – liposuction without the pain or the threat of complications.

We postulate that women who keep shoulder pads pine for those days when shoulder pads reigned supreme.

» CRUD Challenge

What to do with your collection of shoulder pads? You could use a pair to stuff inside a push-up bra to augment your décolletage. Or instead of tissue paper, stuff them into the toes of shoes you are packing for a trip. We recommend that unless you can invent your own purpose, toss them.

› Purse-aholic

Sex in the City celebrated shoe lust in women. A notorious shopper like Imelda Marcos titillated the public with the sheer magnitude of her shoe collection. But the dirty secret? For every shoe acquisition, there's a handbag to match. Not only do we find a surplus of shoes on our clients' closet floors but purses in equal proportion. They multiply as rapidly as fruit flies on a rotting cantaloupe, spilling into drawers, dangling from the backs of doors, their straps and handles in a twisted muddle. Each bag contains its own unique clutter assortment, including solitary hairy cough drops, dry cleaning slips, lip gloss, watches, a fortune in change, fortune cookies and mystery keys.

» CRUD Challenge

If you are a purse-aholic, thinning your considerable collection will be difficult. Start with the more expendable wallets and change purses.

› Blue Velvet

Good things come in unmistakable signature packaging – the velvet box. Unless you count yourself among the jewelry immune, no gift supplies quite the prickle of anticipation as receiving expensive jewelry for a birthday or anniversary. Your mind starts racing. Is it a new watch, bracelet or perhaps a necklace? You remove the wrapping from the gift to behold the velvet box. Even when you've transferred your jewels to another storage receptacle, the tendency is to keep the empty box. We suspect the velvet box is yet a further example of the "too good to throw away" syndrome we encounter with other packaging such as metal cookie tins.

We recently discovered thirty or more empty velvet boxes in a crawl space that had been flooded, but it's more likely you'll find your own in the same dresser drawer where you keep kid gloves, plastic rain bonnets and never used eyeglass cases.

» CRUD Challenge

Use the velvet boxes for actual jewelry storage or give them to your kids to play with. They will invent a clever use for them.

› Fool's Gold

While on the subject of jewelry boxes, let's examine your jewelry collection. We categorize real jewelry as special occasion, usually made out of precious metals and stones with a special sub category devoted to unworn charm bracelets and hideous inherited brooches. Then there is fashion or costume jewelry – all the bling that accessorizes the daily wardrobe. The next classification is the has-beens. Could this be a major category for you? Do you possess single earrings hoping to be reunited with their lost mates? Or twisted chains even the Great Houdini couldn't untangle? Rings missing stones, bracelets with broken catches, watches that have stopped and dented heart-shaped lockets from former boyfriends are all examples. The last category is jewelry you hate. It may be in perfect shape, but it's dated, or the color is putrid. It has other negative associations – like the person who gave it to you. Yet you keep it.

» **CRUD Challenge**

What to do with excess jewelry? Store the expensive stuff you never wear in a safety deposit box. And don't lose the key. Evaluate the un-wearable jewelry. Divide those pieces into groups that are repairable, can be sold for their metal content or can be given away. For you holdouts convinced everything will come back in style, we hope you have room to warehouse it all. But don't you find those screw-back earrings a tad painful after an hour or two?

› Many Happy Returns

Would it be out of the question to suggest that somewhere in your closet you have a shopping bag full of apparel you intended to return but never did? Could some be birthday or Christmas gifts you forgot to mail? Perhaps impulse buying to make up for a lousy day at work resulted in some of these purchases? Might you have exceeded the time period that the store would accept returned merchandise for refund or exchange? Buying is easy, returning unwanted goods to retail stores, catalog companies or home shopping channels is complex and time-consuming. If we hide our shopping faux pas in the bottom of our closets, we can forget them. Amen.

» CRUD Challenge

This is an opportunity to free up premium space and save money. If you can't return the items, consider giving them as presents or donating them to a local charity. Do they have consignment potential?

› It Takes a Lot of Nickels

Open any man's clothes closet. Reach up to the shelf over the hanging rod. Feel around up there. Eventually you'll upset a large cluster of plastic bags overflowing with empty paper rolling tubes. Have you located them yet? They're kind of like a sleeper cell resident in your bedroom. One day they will rise to the occasion, those humble tubes stuffed full of coins, and find their way to the bank for redemption. When a man comes home, his first instinct is to remove the loose change from his pockets. (Women are different. Their idea of saving change is to let it to drop into the netherworlds of their purses, providing an everlasting supply of money for parking meters, tollbooths and vending machines.) But men have jars, drawers, dishes and boxes dedicated to saving change.

People save coins for different objectives. Some treat them as a special fund for a dream vacation or buying a mid-life crisis motorcycle. But no financial institution will allow you to dump a five-gallon jug of pennies at a teller's wicket with the expectation of receiving cash in exchange for your contribution. You have to roll the coins into their appropriate wrappers before you go. Unfortunately, this labor intensive activity is the primary reason change stays out of circulation for decades.

» CRUD Challenge

If you go through the motions of rolling up the coins and cashing them in, you could enjoy a windfall, enough at least for a new putter or a pair of hockey tickets. You will also gain some real estate on the top of your bureau or night table. Perhaps you could drop off the coin collection to a local charity as another option.

› Splatter Proof

Do you keep lots of old battered clothes around? Some clients refer to these garments as painting clothes. Others call them house clothes. This attire escapes the donation bin because the owner finds them comfortable or worthy of sentimental value. Custodians of painting clothes keep them around to perform messy homeowner projects like changing the cat litter or replacing the seal on the toilet. Why risk ruining expensive designer jeans? We don't know how often you paint your home or apartment, but you'd need a 40-year mortgage to rotate through the entire wardrobe of painting clothes we come across. Sometimes we find entire bureaus dedicated to their storage. More often they are consigned to fester in large black or green lawn and leaf bags at the bottom of the closet.

» CRUD Challenge

Pick out one or two specimens for retention. Trash the rest. When clothing reaches the end of the line like these discards, no one else wants them either.

› Down to the Wire

One of our clients shared her theory about wire hangers with us. She says if you hang a few wire hangers in your closet, they multiply as rapidly as ants at a picnic. We see a plague of wire hangers blighting the interiors of closets. If you think about it, humble wire hangers have cultivated certain cult notoriety since Joan Crawford used the hanger as her weapon of choice to inflict her unique brand of discipline. And who could forget the young Dustin Hoffman's "wood or wire" offer to Anne Bancroft in *The Graduate* as a prelude to their tawdry and ill-advised affair?

Few household encounters are reviled by professional organizers as much as confronting a regiment of wire hangers. Wire hangers and their plastic bags are responsible for 25 per cent of the content in bedroom closets. They are no friend of your clothes, no friend indeed. Clothes fall off the hangers and end up in a heap on the floor. If you hang a pair of pants across the midline you will acquire a horizontal crease along your knees that will never disappear. So what if they are free? Your wardrobe deserves better treatment than that.

» CRUD Challenge

What do you do with wire hangers? We conjecture that issue is why people cling to them. You likely are wondering whether your drycleaner will take them off your hands. Pick up the phone and call them. Or find a cleaner that does recycle hangers or look for metal recycling depots in your community. Next time you donate clothes to charity, donate them on the hangers. Keep one hanger and tape it to the undercarriage of your car. You'll have an emergency unlocking tool for the time you lock your keys in the car with the engine running.

› Bedtime Gory

Bedding, like tableware, is an addiction. You need a home equity loan to finance the cost of dressing a bed. For those who love duvets and faux fur blanket throws, there's no form of retail therapy more gratifying than an old-fashioned white sale.

Evaluate your linen closet: sheets, pillows, quilts, mattress covers, bed skirts and pillow protectors for every bed in your house, winter bedding ensembles and corresponding summer ones. What's that, way in the back? Afghans your mother knitted as a wedding present and a dozen or so flannel receiving blankets. Are you taking a fertility drug?

How many rows deep do your one-of-a-kind pillowcases go? Do you still have the twin beds that match the seven sets of twin sheets? Are the comforters on the verge of a breakout?

» CRUD Challenge

Candidates for removal:
- Fitted sheets with shot elastic.
- Anything that requires ironing.
- Shams without matching bedspreads.

Donate what's salvageable and recycle the rest. Humane societies and other animal rescue organizations always need sheets and towels. Save one white sheet for an emergency ghost costume.

› Tee'd Off

Sometime during the mid-1960s the T-shirt went from an all-white, three-to-a-package underwear staple, to the human equivalent of a billboard.

Open the dresser drawers of any North American male, 10 to 65, and the plethora of cotton and polyester blends commemorating everything from a Tiny Tim concert to a sixth grade class reunion will overwhelm you. Combing though someone's T-shirt drawer presents a walk down memory lane. You might find anything from "My parents went on vacation to the Galapagos and all I got was this lousy T-shirt" to "I'm having an out of money experience." Every protest march, political race, cartoon character and walk-to-cure a disease is commemorated with a T-shirt. After a couple of decades, the shirts succumb to over-washing and fading. They do stay the same size, even if the owners don't.

» CRUD Challenge

Dedicated collectors feel violated if even a single T-shirt eludes their grasp. One severely space-challenged client with a keen interest in transportation owned hundreds of shirts, many in tatters. He refused to part with a single one. While T-shirts may be appropriate attire for leisure activities like sports, rock concerts, camping and cookouts, they don't play well at the office or formal occasions. Subject them to the same scrutiny that you apply to the rest of your wardrobe. Be honest. Does it still cover your stomach? Would your children be mortified if they saw you wearing that souvenir from the Cheech and Chong concert?

› Dress for Less

One of the underrated Las Vegas attractions is a visit to the

Liberace Museum. Forget about the $250 a ticket nightclub extravaganzas, the non-stop games of chance and the more-than-you-can-eat 24-hour buffets. Nestled off the Strip in an unassuming mall lies a shrine to excess, where not only are you treated to Liberace's twinkling pianos and cars, you also receive a virtual tour of his clothes closet, narrated by Lee himself, on a continuous video loop. Speaking from the grave, he proudly draws your attention to his 700 dress shirts, countless pairs of shoes and other assorted articles. At one point he describes his three wardrobes as thin, fat and impossible. Most of our clients don't possess the number of suits that Liberace owned, but we do see a great deal of size variation in their closets.

In a recent study, two thirds of the women surveyed admitted to buying clothes a size too small in the hope of losing weight. The research also revealed that each woman in the study owned an average of 14 items, such as jeans, blouses, skirts, dresses and shoes, which were never worn. You may not be a Liberace, but there is a direct connection between bloated closets and behaviors like yo-yo dieting and the unaccountable suspension of disbelief associated with the subject of future weight loss. You may lose the pounds, but when you are trimmer, would you be caught dead in that Nehru jacket? Would you wear a one-piece jumpsuit? Spandex micro-skirts don't flatter anyone born before the first Gulf War. No matter how much you paid, there's no room for the unworn garments you hoard.

» CRUD Challenge

Women love to shop for clothes. Unfortunately very little thought is given to storage. Many take the position that the closet will expand infinitely to embrace everything they own. How do you know if you've bought one too many items? Is the racking system collapsing? Do you set your alarm 30 minutes earlier than necessary because your closet is so densely packed? Do you find yourself repeating the mantra "I have nothing to wear" as you stare blankly at a rack of dresses, suits and sportswear?

When you've reached your personal saturation point, here are some suggestions:

- Get someone whose opinion you trust to help you.

  Try stuff on. Be ruthless.
- Sell, consign, donate or recycle.
- Hold a clothing swap. Refresh and chuck at the same time.

› The Ties that Bind

Remember the Father's Days of yore? Every Dad expected a tie, received a tie and had to pretend to be surprised and thrilled with the gift. Men had so many ties back then. Ties were constantly going in and out of fashion based on color, pattern and width. Men even installed tie racks in their closets (one of the very first closet organizing products). But there was also a dark side to all this neckwear. For many, wearing a tie every day symbolized a kind of corporate wage-slave culture. The first thing a man would do upon his return home from work was remove the offending garment.

Many business people, politicians and professionals still wear them. But the majority of the population wears a tie only at special occasions, job interviews and graduations. The real death blow to the necktie was the revelation that ties worn by physicians spread infection.

» CRUD Challenge

In your personal tie collection there must be a hefty representation of solids, stripes and patterns in both the wide and narrow varieties. Are there any decorated in Warner Bros. cartoon figures? There may also be a bow tie or two from the last formal affair. Purge. Then review the tie tacks and tie clips in the dish on your dresser. They are easy to find. You keep them with the cufflinks you still have for the French-cuff dress shirts you no longer own.

› Always a Bridesmaid

One of our favorite websites and an inspiration for our own Good Riddance Virtual Clutter Museum is www.uglydress.com only surpassed by the brilliant www.burntfoodmuseum.com celebrating culinary disasters.

Several decades and divorces after your stint as a bridesmaid, you hang on to that ruffled bridesmaid frock in a ghastly pastel shade meant to flatter everyone from a size zero to a 3X. Stuffed full of tissue in a garment bag, it takes up the same amount of space as five stunning Armani pantsuits. Imagine the Queen Mary berthed in your clothes closet. Have you questioned why it is still there? The bride probably doesn't have her white wedding gown, since she moved to a commune in Taos to practice reflexology. You can't think you are going to alter it to wear to some elegant fundraiser or on New Year's Eve. After all, does anyone look good in peach?

We congratulate the modern brides of today who allow black to be worn by the wedding party. That way, when you plunk down $400 for a dress, you have a chance of wearing it again for something other than a costume.

» CRUD Challenge

Categorize bridesmaid dresses under clothing saved for sentiment. Add camp sweatshirts, Girl Scout uniforms and your first training bra. If you have the space, keep them for the memory. If not, send the ugly dress to another galaxy.

CHAPTER 11

CHILD'S PREY

ROTTING UNEATEN LUNCHES & OTHER HORRORS IN YOUR KIDS' ROOMS

We get calls from distressed mothers and fathers who want to hang a condemned sign on the door of their kids' bedrooms, semblances of the remains of a dollar store in Oklahoma after a twister has struck. Early on, children form attachments to their toys, costumes, books and media. If you suggest parting with anything to these children, you can provoke a reaction that calls for earplugs.

The most common complaint we get is the substitution of the floor for a closet. Clean or dirty, clothing ends up on the floor. Toys, followed by art supplies, usurp most of the space in the house.

Schoolwork, treasured beyond reason, adds to the clutter. You don't have to save every vocabulary test your daughter ever took. Her college degree provides evidence of her academic prowess.

Sometimes we work in kids' rooms that contain so many tanks and cages of exotic animals, you'd swear you were in the Amazon.

You think that they will grow out of it. But what if your 20-something daughter is still living at home amongst her horsemanship ribbons, 47 pairs of designer jeans and hair extensions? And what if she still has no awareness of the chaos that ensnares her? You could lead by example by doing a number on your own bedroom, which may be preferable to screaming matches and slamming doors. Kids' rooms are one of the reasons scientists invented tranquilizers.

› 99 Bottles of Beer on the Wall

This section targets the late adolescent males, 18 to 24, who have recently attained legal drinking status. Bookshelves and dresser tops that formerly housed books, model airplanes, Disneyland photos and pictures of sports heroes, have given way to rows of empty glass liquor and beer bottles. Although the display suggests a machismo in certain circles, it may signal a new recruit for AA.

» CRUD Challenge

Dig out that recycling container and help him avoid a life spent in the 12-step program. You might convince the collector to cooperate by telling him he can keep the money the bottles fetch at the depot.

› Refrigerator Art

Mothers, if you save every crayon streak, finger painting and doodle produced by your budding artist, you will need to move to a bigger house. This is no reflection on either you or your child's potential to be the next Picasso. This is just a warning.

Once the kids go to school, daycare and camp, the artwork torrent will reach flooding levels.

How many Popsicle stick sculptures, shell-encrusted photo frames and ceramic dog-pile look-alikes will it take for you to comprehend that these treasures can usurp all your bookshelf, countertop and coffee table surfaces? Restrict yourself to the best of the best.

» CRUD Challenge

Designate one large see-through storage container for artwork storage. Select one or two outstanding pieces from each school year or time period. Be strong. Discarding a multitude of construction paper art projects does not render you a child abuser.

› Trophy Lives

While we are on the sensitive topic of children's accomplishments, let's tackle another major invader – athletic medals and trophies. There is so much shiny metal adorning the rooms of North America's adolescent population that you need to don sunglasses before entering. Now we do not want to appear too cynical here. However, we remember a time when these awards were bestowed on the actual winners, and possibly runners up, in athletic events and tournaments. These days any child who participates in any sports activity walks away with a medal, plaque or trophy. They get them for showing up. All of this recognition will set them up for disappointment in later life. How are they going to feel when no one rewards them for coming to work on time?

» CRUD Challenge

Edit – at least every few years. Preserve the ones that actually recognize accomplishment, such as winning the 100-meter freestyle or placing first in the spelling bee. Leave room in your child's memory container for a few more. Get a buy-in from your son or daughter on this issue.

› By Jiminy

Jiminy Cricket was the most influential insect of all time. An entire generation learned how to spell E-N-C-Y-C-L-O-P-E-D-I-A, thanks to Jiminy Cricket's musical rendition of *Encyclopedia* on the Mickey Mouse Club television show. Talk about an albatross. The once respected and undisputed repository of factual material has slid from grace. At one time parents considered it a sacred obligation to purchase a whole set of hefty tomes plus their annual updates. Door-to-door salespeople employed high-pressure tactics foretelling a dismal and limited future for the children of families who refused to buy their books. A home encyclopedia also meant parents no longer had to drive their kids to the library to complete assignments. Today, who would look up information in a set of books filled with

35-year-old outdated information? As organizers we see sets of encyclopedias all the time in the same rooms that are equipped with computers, iPods and cellphone chargers. These kids have access to the world's databanks in the same place they lay their heads at night.

» CRUD Challenge

There is a ton of emotional baggage around books and in particular around encyclopedias. Used book dealers inform us there is no value in these old books and no market. Don't get sucked in by gauzy memories of ripping reads on rainy weekend afternoons. These really do need to go. Remove them from your children's rooms so the kids have the shelf space to display their own treasures and obsessions. Relocate the encyclopedias to a guest room or basement playroom, if you must, but the best solution is to recycle.

› Non-Plushed

Calling all allergy sufferers!

Stuffed toys take over and occupy every inch of shelf, dresser and closet space. The menagerie multiplies so rapidly there is no room left for sleeping on the bed. When the hoarding of stuffed animals spills into adulthood, alarm bells should be going off. We have witnessed grown women hyperventilate at the suggestion of donating a fuzzy lion cub or penguin. We suppose that – like living pets – they offer a source of unconditional love.

» CRUD Challenge

Thank Walt Disney for your life-long attachment to plush toys. Start new addictions more appropriate to your age and station in life. Consider cosmetic surgery and anti-depressants as substitutes. You will sleep better when you are not sharing your mattress with 35 stuffed German Shepherds. There might even be room for your husband or boyfriend.

› Bootie Call

Babyhood was a unique time when as a parent you exercised complete control over the lives of your offspring. No one demanded your car keys or ran up cellphone bills. Saving baby clothes transports you back to an innocent and happier period when a crisis was spit-up on a new silk blouse and mommy was a superpower. The experience is rarely repeated. Rose-colored memories have blotted out the chronic sleep deprivation and stretch marks that also characterized those times.

We have witnessed many hard-nosed female executives dissolve into tears when downsizing their adult child's infant wardrobe. They cite, between sniffles, many legitimate reasons to cling to little caps, sweaters, bathing trunks and sandals. "That was her Toto costume from *The Wizard of Oz*." The list goes on. Baby clothes are one the most contentious forms of household clutter. When you factor in siblings, only drastic measures will suffice.

» CRUD Challenge

If one pair of overalls is all you've salted away from your child's early years, skip this section. But if your eyes are welling at the thought of jettisoning any article of clothing smaller than 6X, stay tuned. Select a few items to save for posterity. Cherish the memory, not the object. Limit yourself to one storage bin per child. Otherwise, consign or donate to a women's transition house. You might liberate so much space you could surrender your storage locker.

" But I need to keep all my plastic grocery bags for my friend when she visits this summer. She always brings her Shih Tzu. "

CRUD logic for stockpiling plastic bags.

CHAPTER 12

BROTHER CAN YOU
SPARE A ROOM?

S pare rooms, the unwanted step-children in the house, are the most cluttered areas in a residence according to a 2008 report by Australian Josh Fear in *Stuff Happens: Unused things cluttering up our homes.*

Ponder what might be occupying your extra bedroom. Could that be the room where your grandmother's antique furniture resides? Hmmm. What's that over there? The old computer untouched since 1996, Christmas stuff that didn't quite make it to the basement, someone's faded shorts and Hawaiian shirt, costumes from Halloweens past and a banker's box full of cordless phone apparatus. Are you getting the picture?

Fated to serve as a halfway house for discarded household goods, the spare room functions as a personal panic room for stuff. You stash all the piles and unsightly messes there, moments before your company arrives. You get partial usage out of the room as an occasional flop for a visiting out-of-town relative. But mostly it's the room you hope nobody will stumble into at a party, mistaking it for the bathroom.

The space has the potential to be a sewing center, workout room, office, play room, media room or a student rental. But it's been three years since junior packed his bags and the spare room is still a holding tank.

› Which Craft?

For the dedicated crafter, one hobby is never enough. We have worked with dozens of talented, enthusiastic creative types who struggle to control their craft supplies. Quilters top the list – no single scrap of fabric is expendable. Even their cars are equipped with a Global Positioning System capable of locating a fabric store within a 25-mile radius.

When the passion for needle arts spills into sewing, patterns add to the clutter. Knitting and crocheting add major contributions in the way of supplies. Yarn exudes its own hypnotic effect.

We have beheld the remains of abandoned jewelry and soap-making enterprises, stained glass, china painting and beeswax candle experiments. A more recent phenomenon is the proliferation of scrapbooking. Clients invest a small fortune in albums, cropping tools, carrying cases and embellishments. What this all adds up to is a storage nightmare.

While many of these pastimes are still actively pursued, most have been relegated to "been there, done that." We classify much of what is languishing in opaque plastic bags in the upper regions of the closet as UFOs – Unfinished Objects, projects never completed, like the blanket you were crocheting for the baby who just graduated from law school.

» CRUD Challenge

If your sewing machine, husband and dog went missing and you are leaning toward offering a reward for the sewing machine, you have work to do. Open those plastic bins, drawers and boxes. Do you still derive pleasure from these activities? Parting with craft supplies is a complex process laden with guilt, considering that investment in supplies might rival the cost of a college education. All the while, the voice in your head is whispering that you will complete those projects "when I have the time." This is an 800-pound gorilla you're dealing with. Be consoled. Many non-profit societies, seniors' centers and schools, and even your craft buddies, would love to take your excess off your hands.

› Excess Baggage

Why is it that when people buy replacement luggage they don't sell, donate or throw away their old, dilapidated suitcases? This is serious baggage, a real elephant in the middle of the room. How many of these relics can you claim? Would you ever travel with molded plastic avocado green suitcases with stick-on initials, given to you as a graduation present? They surpass airline baggage weight restrictions when they are empty. How many pieces do you own without wheels or telescoping handles? Don't overlook the inherited plaid garment bags, duffel bags, the trunk from summer camp and the half dozen shoulder straps separated from their carry-on bags.

» CRUD Challenge

Toss what would humiliate you checking into a hotel. If you store baby clothes and your children are applying for post-graduate fellowships, make this a double-play – donate container and contents. While you are at it, don't forget the luggage carts on wheels.

"They have significant historical value."

*CRUD logic for saving a worthless collection
of wooden carvings picked up on vacation.*

› Wrapture

Have you noticed the exalted level to which gift wrap has risen? Today we package presents in a myriad of ways: in cloth bags, tissue paper and decorative boxes as well as in the traditional standbys – wrapping paper and ribbons. Christmas wrapping has a category of its own.

Perhaps you save the wrapping from presents received with the good intention of reusing it on some future gift. Once unfurled, those half-used, three-foot tubes are a storage nightmare. Most of them are shoved into the closet and usually fall down every time you open the bi-folds. They collapse in a heap, preventing you from accessing the ironing board, vacuum cleaner or other difficult-to-store household necessities.

Face it. You simply can't resist the temptation of the unblemished, starched appeal of a new roll.

» CRUD Challenge

Consider plastic containers to corral these unruly cylinders.

Take inventory of gift bags, unused wrapping paper, tissue and cellophane, scotch tape, bows, elastics and enclosures. Divide that by the number of people you will shop for in a one-year period. That way you can arrive at a figure that predicts how many gifts you will need to purchase annually. If your gift wrap collection exceeds that number to the power of four, EDIT. Start with the really wrinkled sheets. Then heave the flattened gift boxes with the names of stores that went out of business at least 10 years ago.

› Gag Mechanism

There ought to be a special place in hell for the inventors of gag and novelty items. You either purchase or receive them to mark with a little levity special occasions like major birthdays that end in zeros, retirement parties and company holiday gift exchanges. Gag gifts are given with the intent to embarrass and humiliate the recipient, relying on advanced age, sexual dysfunction or incontinence to produce laughs. What could be more hilarious than an over-the-hill diaper on your 30th birthday? Often these presents are equipped with irritating soundtracks. Like many under-appreciated gifts, there is no obligation to keep them.

» CRUD Challenge

Who has not found glee in the strategic placement of a flatulence sound-alike cushion at some point in his life? We recommend a backyard burial or insertion in a time capsule for all gifts of this ilk. Future generations will conclude that the decline and fall of our civilization can be traced to obsessions with erectile dysfunction treatments and squirting doorbells.

› Picture This

If professional organizers bestowed sainthood on products, the digital camera would be a leading contender. Although they have spawned an industry of their own in accessories and printing paraphernalia, they represent our greatest hope for a clutter-free future. So what if the images are eating up our hard drives.

No household equivalent of the Centers for Disease Control monitors the progress of the photograph plague. For those of you too young to remember, before the advent of the digital camera, people took photos with equipment that required film. The film was developed and returned in paper envelopes, complete with negatives. For a small additional charge, you received an extra set of prints to share with family and friends.

Fast forward a decade or two. What became of all of those photos? We get the desperation call. Our clients agonize at the idea of wading into shoeboxes, steamer trunks, desk drawers and cartons loaded with pictures – the duplicates still in the envelopes awaiting forwarding. The framed photos, class and team pictures crowd the sideboard. Others don't even make it to frames. The anguish extends to albums as well.

You may be the custodian of the family history. Albums bequeathed to you by deceased relatives take up so much room there is no place to display your own books or artwork. Nobody knows who most of the people are in the pictures. How many boxes of slide carousels can you count? Do you still own a slide projector with a working bulb? Are there any canisters of 8mm home movies? You might even unearth the screen and projector.

» CRUD Challenge

Stop hyperventilating now. We warn clients not to embark on a photo purging/organizing jaunt unless they have a long stretch of idle time to devote to the task. While the lion's shares of snapshots reside in an extra bedroom or storage closet, we know many more are hidden in stashes around the house. They pop up everywhere – junk drawers, glove compartments, kids' backpacks, etc.

What criteria should be employed in the decision-making process?

- Discard any picture that does not show you to your best advantage – any pictures where your hair looks bad, you are not at your ideal weight or you are wearing an outfit that would earn you a guest appearance on Extreme Makeover.
- All sunsets look alike.
- Ditch all the duplicates and near duplicates.
- Nix pictures of your friends' babies from 20 years ago, exes of both sexes and anyone wearing a cap and gown.
- Digitize pictures you want to preserve.

Now you understand our reverence for the digital camera.

› Gift Emporium

The proliferation of dollar stores across the land has spawned a peculiar phenomenon. The merchandise is so cheap people plunk down cash at an alarming rate. How else to explain the presence of so many new plastic cheese graters, basketball sets and collapsible umbrellas stored in a single location, usually the spare bedroom? Nor can you heap blame solely on the dollar store. Conditioning has honed our instinct to grab anything in quantity that we consider a bargain. Whether we are in the mall, a big box store or a liquidation outlet, the 97-cents bin grabs our attention.

These excessive mini-shopping sprees result in bedrooms cum gift stores with stockpiles of gifts awaiting occasions. The greatest proponents of gift caches are mothers of school age children who spend every weekend chauffeuring children to and from birthday parties. After a few frantic dashes into a big box store on the way to the festivities to find a last minute gift, women adopt a stockpiling approach.

This is where it starts to get ugly. The shopping continues unabated. After a few months, the piles grow. A binky box or tickle trunk morphs into giant plastic containers. The storage room becomes a warehouse, minus the forklifts. You can no longer locate those party favors you thought were so appealing. Those vegetable scrapers and the waffle iron you were going to re-gift? Where did they go? You don't even know what you have. Then you are back to square one. You are back to buying something on the way.

» CRUD Challenge

Shop in your own store first. Whittle down your inventory and extricate yourself from dollar store excursions.

› Shady Characters

You can peg a home's vintage by its lighting. Interior lighting, like everything else, has a lifespan. Renovation or redecorating calls for new lighting fixtures. But what do you do with the old lighting, still in working order?

Our clients are often faced with a glut of floor and table lamps, fluorescent tubes, dismantled track lights and ceiling fixtures. Lighting is a storage nightmare – it has wires that rarely remain passively coiled and unwieldy shades that don't conform to the shapes of standard rectangular boxes.

Did we mention bulbs? Bulbs come in every measure of power from restaurant menu blindness – providing the illumination equivalent to one Chanukah candle – to KGB interrogation intensity. Light bulbs break easily, shattering into thousands of shards of glass. Add in switch plates, lamp bases, harps, finials and chandelier crystals. We advocate a lights out policy for your excess wattage.

» CRUD Challenge

Here is your lighting hit list:

- Swag lamps. Popular in the 70s, swag lamps decorated the games table and kitchen island.
- Pole lamps. Chrome, brass or plastic. These rotating globes of light are useless unless you want to highlight the cobwebs on the ceiling.
- Chianti bottle lamps. These were early attempts to recycle glass – not a justification for keeping them.
- Metal desk lights that clip on shelves. They topple down and burn you when you need them most.
- Strings of colored lights. Whether they are the acres of burned out holiday lights or novelties like chili peppers, chuck them.

- Halogen torchière floor lamps. Recalled as fire hazards by the Consumer Product Safety Commission in 2004. Why are you keeping them?

Do keep a goose-neck cordless work light, an essential tool in downsizing. It wraps around poles and furniture – you will need one when you excavate the dark holes in the basement.

› Bored Games

Baby boomers grew up on a steady diet of spongy white bread, test patterns and board games, courtesy of Milton Bradley and Parker Brothers – the Nintendo and Electronic Arts of their day. Some original editions are collectors' items and can fetch impressive sums on auction sites.

But many boomers, intent on recreating the nuclear family ambience of the mid 20th century, continue to purchase board games, forgetting their kids are children of the Internet who can have an interactive play experience by connecting with other players in Bulgaria or Iceland. Board games, while tactile and moderately engaging, can't compete with the intensity of today's graphic-rich electronic counterparts.

At best, the board games get dragged along on family vacations to remote cabins without power and cellphone reception. In the long summer evenings, the family plays rounds of Scrabble or Mille Bornes by flashlight. When the week ends, the board games, some hardly played and others in tatters, are interred in storage, remaining there for another decade or so, until the experiment is repeated upon a crop of grandchildren.

» CRUD Challenge

Board games loom large in the nostalgia department.

When you are ready to deal with them, consider a mask as protection from dust storm that will ensue when these boxes are purged. What to keep, what to discard? Open the boxes. Are all the parts there? We mean the scorecards, dice, racks, tokens, spinners and cards, even the board itself. How appealing would a game of Monopoly be minus the houses or hotels? This should not take you all day. Keep one or two favorite games in the event of a power failure.

› Birthday Cards

In our view, birthday cards are ephemeral tokens. If displayed on the mantel or bulletin board, they should be removed periodically to make room for someone else's moment in the spotlight. We wish.

Walk into any cluttered home and we will guarantee the resident has saved every birthday card ever received. This is not some isolated phenomenon, but as commonplace as keeping old issues of Reader's Digest. We find them in plastic bags, shoeboxes and in those decorative faux leather storage boxes that go on sale every January. These same clients are likely to also hoard get well, anniversary, Christmas, retirement, wedding, new baby, Mother's Day and graduation cards. Depending on the age of the recipient, these collections mount up.

We've heard all the excuses: a need to reply, a record of the address, plan to use the pictures for making your own cards or art projects. People who keep stuff like this seldom have time to follow through on their good intentions.

» CRUD Challenge

How many souvenirs do you need as a reminder that the older you get the less attractive you become? Our favorite find proclaimed: "You are so old. Why aren't you dead?"

Birthday cards score in the toxic zone of the CRUD factor because of their emotional connection. We urge you to toss without perusing because reading the content will slow you down. (Also good advice for dealing with heaps of letters and old photos.) You will probably insist on going through each and every one. Don't say we didn't warn you.

In that case, check the envelopes for five-dollar bills or uncashed checks you missed the first time round – when you focused on opening the present not the card.

CHAPTER 13

A HEAVY DARK LOAD

LAUNDRY ROOM CLUTTER YOU CAN'T BLEACH AWAY

If you are fortunate enough to have a dedicated area in your home for laundry, count yourself blessed. If the laundry room is on the same floor as your kitchen or bedrooms, consider yourself doubly fortunate. Your iron and ironing board, drying racks and laundry baskets belong there as well as extra light bulbs, cleaning products, rug shampooers and household tools.

Unfortunately, over time this pristine environment loses some of its cachet. Other items enter its domain, and never leave – end rolls of wallpaper, designer shopping bags, catering trays never returned, a myriad of unreliable miracle cleaners and multiple copies of expired Yellow Pages. By now there is no room to fold even a humble handkerchief.

› Solitary Confinement

Single socks! Why do their mates vanish? Some heap blame on the washer, while others credit the dryer. We personally favor the family dog, given the canine penchant for inhaling and tasting human attire, the smellier the better. Regardless of why they become separated, there is a simple solution. As mothers, it took us years to figure this out. Always buy the same socks. Never deviate.

» CRUD Challenge

Instead of waiting the return of the prodigal socks – also applies to mittens or anything that comes in pairs – do something bold. Dump them. Start over.

› Rag Hag

Have you ever said "Oh, I can use that as a rag?" How many rags can one person use in a lifetime? Mothers have the biggest rag collections. We've worked with mothers who agonize over giving away little Tommy's size 3X pajamas. Even though Tommy is now 27, they ultimately decide to keep the threadbare pajama bottoms as a rag. This satisfies two sets of needs: nostalgic Moms get to keep the treasured garment as well as re-purpose it for continued use.

> *" I have to keep all that we find because I'm going to make a quilt."*
>
> CRUD logic from a woman reluctant to
> donate a single scrap of unused fabric.

» CRUD Challenge

Rags are more environmentally friendly than a roll of paper towels, but too many rags produce serious storage issues. Reduce the rags to a manageable level – no more than a plastic bagful. Give the rest to the local high school for a car wash fundraiser.

› Curtains!

When you moved in five years ago you replaced the window treatments. So why are those drab beige drapery panels and sheers occupying center stage in your cramped linen closet or laundry room? The same goes for those metal Venetian blinds that need to be restrung and the window shades that refuse to retract on command. Are you holding on to floral printed curtains that once matched long-gone bedspreads and slipcovers?

» CRUD Challenge

Get rid of old drapery, blinds, etc. and at the same time the collection of curtain rods, hooks, valances, finials and tie-backs. Donate or recycle.

› Nature Abhors a Vacuum Part

When clients replace their vacuum cleaners, they neglect to dispose of the attachments from their old machines. In homes where multiple vacuums are commonplace – hand-held for quick cleanups, wet-dry versions for the workshop, electric brooms and the venerable upright or canister types – the spare parts and niche tools multiply exponentially. Almost every vacuum cleaner requires its own proprietary set of bags, all letter-coded and guaranteed not to fit any other vacuum you might ever buy. Do not forget to factor in the extra nozzles and hoses.

» CRUD Challenge

Most homes or apartments have inadequate storage for the vacuum cleaner. Vacuums are stuffed wherever space can be found – on top of a pile of winter boots in the hall closet or in the corner of the dining room. All the more reason to be vigilant about those vestigial parts. How many of them have you ever actually used? If you go to laminate, you can get rid of the entire lot.

› Battery Cram

Batteries are indispensable sources of energy that power everything from cellphones to sex toys. They come in an array of sizes and composition, some re-chargeable and others that go lifeless in seconds. Some people dedicate entire drawers to them, but usually batteries wind up in many locations around the house such as in the dog's bowl or the vegetable crisper.

Our issues are not with the packaged batteries, but the discards, neglected because no one knows how to recycle them. Or it's too much trouble to find out if they've expired, so they remain in limbo.

» CRUD Challenge

Declare today battery round-up day. Get everyone in your household to empty their nightstands, junk drawers, desk drawers, wicker baskets and other stashes for small objects. Retire the duds and salvage the ones that will operate a Game Boy. You might save enough money from this endeavor to treat yourself to a pedicure.

" My father collected these tennis balls whenever he took the family dog for a walk."

CRUD logic for shipping a box of 85 lifeless and grubby tennis balls across the country.

CHAPTER 14

CELLAR STALKS
THE SCARIEST PLACES IN YOUR HOME

Does the thought of exploring the nether regions of your basement invoke the foreboding theme music from Jaws? If so, make sure you go accompanied. The basement is a subterranean purgatory for the all the underused and forgotten fragments of daily living you don't want to face.

For some people, the fear of spiders renders them helpless, but for most it's the fear of confronting the buried bodies. While the public areas of your home may pass scrutiny, the basement resembles the town dump. We had one client who kicked stuff down the stairs while crying out "whoopsie" every time she came across an unwanted item.

Another client had built a bomb shelter in the home during the height of the Cold War. It still contained food to feed the family in the event of an attack by the former USSR.

We sub-divide the basement into several categories:

• Unlikely to be repaired zone. This includes the acutely neglected, such as chairs that need reupholstering and badminton nets that require mending.
• Inheritance zone. This area holds the family heirlooms like rattan bar stools you were too intimidated to say no to

when your parents moved to a retirement community.
Loot from two or three generations often resides here. The
yellowed newsprint wrapped around the heirlooms
advertises millinery and notions.

- Saving for the kids' zone. Toys, games, books, schoolwork,
complete sets of dishes and flatware reside here. NOTE:
The chances of your children wanting any of these are
slim to none.

- Personal history zone. Where you store all of life's mementos
like your lifesaving badge from camp or the matchbooks
from your wedding reception.

› Life would be great if it weren't for other people

Items you've been storing for other people can hog a major
share of the space in your basement. Sometimes these people
move away and disappear from your life altogether. You are left
holding the bag, or shall we say bags.

That rusted bed frame and headboard once belonged to
a former roommate with whom you lost touch 15 years ago.
Those cross country skis and poles? They belong to your cousin
who lives on a houseboat in Miami.

We recently worked with a woman whose daughter was in
her 30s and lived 3000 miles away. Her mother had saved the
daughter's treasures including special commemorative beer cans
from the 1970s.

You have enough of your own rubbish to contend with: ditch the forgotten trappings of others.

» CRUD Challenge

Ignore those guilty feelings. Pick up the telephone and explain to family and friends that you are in the process of purging your home. Tell them you have identified the items that belong to them. Ask them to arrange for pickup by a clear-cut deadline. If the individual is unable to comply with your timetable, explain you will arrange for disposal.

Off-site storage is a major growth industry today. Millions of people are paying handsomely for storage lockers. Think of how much money you've saved your friends and relatives over the years by storing their unframed posters, old checkbooks, quilted bedspreads and postcard collections. Don't chicken out. Remember, if they're family, they'll get over it. They still have to talk to you.

› Boxed In

Here is the second really big tip that will accelerate the process. Get rid of the boxes. You know the ones we mean. All new appliances, electronics or tools come in boxes. Most include packing inserts to protect the items through shipping. Many of our clients save boxes in case the new device needs returning. When you consider all the kitchen appliances, home entertainment options and office automation products that share our living quarters, we are talking about a lot of boxes.

When we run into these cardboard cities in our clients' basements, we probe: is the item pictured on the box still in the home? How long have you owned it? Often times we discover that the cordless phones and TVs have been replaced several times. Nonetheless, the packaging hangs on.

We also believe there is another reason why people cling so tenaciously to these boxes. They are just too substantial to throw away.

» CRUD Challenge

Fortunately, we recently learned about an electronics retailer in our area that will take packaging off your hands when you purchase a new or replacement product. Check with retailers in your area to see if they have a recycling program before you buy your next appliance.

Determine which boxes belong to the products that are still under warranty. Keep those, but not indefinitely. Invest in a heavy duty knife or box cutter. Chop up and flatten the boxes for the recycling bin. This activity has been described as cathartic by some. To those who object to this paper massacre on the grounds that things break and do have to be sent back to the manufacturer, we remind you that no one fixes anything anymore. If it breaks, you usually get a new one.

› Time Wounds All Heels

From the removal of inflamed tonsils to knee or hip replacements, many of us require a hospital stay and some form of aid or equipment to promote recovery. But why do so many people restored to health keep medical souvenirs for decades in their basements? We mean crutches, casts, bedpans, canes, walkers, wheelchairs, and in extreme cases, the offending body parts themselves like gallstones or umbilical cords.

» CRUD Challenge

There is nothing quite as boring as listening to someone else's play-by-play description of his or her experience with the medical system – the length of the procedure, the importance of the surgeon, the bad food (and small portions) and the mistreatment by the insensitive staff.

Who wants to be reminded of all of that? Put this helpful equipment in the hands of people who really need it. Donate the functional supplies to a local clinic or Red Cross. You really don't need those kidney stones in a jar either.

› Platter Matter

In an age where thousands of your favorite songs can be downloaded to devices the size of a credit card, why are record albums so revered? If anything has been banished to the foulest regions of the basement, it is these reminders of youthful times that rarely, if ever, are in the mint condition expected by serious collectors. Rather they give off an essence of mildew, are warped, scratched and missing their paper liners. The covers are faded and dog-eared. Since they take up so much valuable storage space, they are often the objects of contention between spouses. Often there is no phonograph in the home on which to play them.

» CRUD Challenge

If your partner is the guilty party, try saying things like, "You know we could fit a pool table in the space currently being occupied with your British Invasion LPs."

› Out of Order

In our basement forays we run into kitchen appliances of the small and not-currently-working variety – coffee makers, toasters, microwave ovens, can openers, coffee grinders, mixers, blenders, Crock-Pots and food processors. We also stumble across the occasional electric frying pan, waffle maker, bread maker or espresso machine.

Add to the mix power tools, hair-dryers, fans, vacuums, TVs, stereos, irons, computers and floor polishers.

Basements provide breeding grounds for un-repaired devices. What is break-even point when it comes to fixing or tossing? You may be deluding yourself that you will repair the defective appliance in your spare time. Or, you may believe it is merely obtaining the right part that is coming between you and a fully functional DVD player. Some of our clients insist on keeping broken appliances as spares in the event their replacements go bad.

» CRUD Challenge

Fix them or lose them. They won't nurse themselves back to health. Ditch the ones that cost under $150 and repair the more expensive ones. Check your local recycling guidelines for methods of responsible disposal.

› Natural Wonders

Frequently we find rocks, shells, driftwood, pinecones and containers of sand in dresser drawers, on bookshelves and mantels. We refer to them as natural wonders because we naturally wonder why people keep them. They are the freebies of the souvenir world, designed to take you back to the carefree time you spent camping or sunning on a beach. Perhaps you removed petrified wood from a national park. Shame on you.

Once you get the natural wonders home, they don't match your furniture and décor. So they're shipped to the basement. If truth be told, you probably can't recall where they came from in the first place. Don't bother wracking your brain. You can always get another rock.

» CRUD Challenge

The good news is that these collectables are easy to get rid of – right outside the door or on a trip to the park. Restore them to Mother Nature.

› Face the Music

Most of us, as children, learn to play a musical instrument at some level. For the talented, the lessons pave the way to a lifelong passion that is lucrative and creative.

For the non-musically inclined, studying music produces an opposite effect – power struggles, boredom and agony. If there is to be any return to peace and harmony in the home, parents of the tone deaf must be disabused of their grandiose notions of siring a child prodigy. Mercifully, once realized, said instruments of torture get packed away into the bowels of the building: trumpets in their protective cases, the electronic keyboard purchased one Christmas, expensive drum sets, speakers, amps and guitars, guitars, guitars. The result is a basement littered with the remains of a fortune spent on music lessons.

Lots of teens have short-lived entanglements with rock bands, most of which never make it out of the garage – assuming your garage has enough space for rehearsing a four-piece ensemble. These groups generally disband once they realize their prospects for a recording contract are dim. Meanwhile, the instruments, charts and sound equipment hang on.

Another way instruments intrude is via inheritance from ancestors in the old country. We recently had to empty an entire room of balalaikas.

» CRUD Challenge

Divesting yourself of a musical instrument feels a little like throwing away a former self. In the purging continuum, this falls in the moderate to intense range. Check the condition of the instruments. Donate to friends or organizations or sell on-line. Plan one more jam session before you say goodbye.

We need to inform you about the one instrument that nobody wants – the organ. When we are evaluating a home for a downsizing project, we despair when we recognize the familiar hulking shape in the living or dining room. Senior centers, churches and schools have all rejected the organ. Give yourself a long lead time or pray for divine intervention. There's not much demand for accordions either.

› The Sorcerer's Apprentice

One of the most beloved and enduring film images is that of Mickey Mouse outnumbered by legions of brooms carrying and emptying pails of water. Just when he is to meet his demise by drowning, he is rescued by his terror-inspiring master, the sorcerer. We experience a similar drowning sensation when we enter a basement area to discover a caucus of old and dirty mops and brooms, surrounded by dustpans and plastic buckets. More up-to-date disposable or environmentally friendly models have replaced these cleaning implements. The foam rubber sponges have hardened into fossils. The brooms' bristles are mostly missing. So, why are they there?

We figure their size and shape make clearance inconvenient. It is not like mops fit in a garbage can. You have to take them to a recycling center or find a dumpster behind a commercial establishment where you can toss them when the coast is clear.

» CRUD Challenge

Chew on this. What would you do if Oprah made an unannounced visit to your basement and stumbled on your mop collection? It might destroy any possibility of your making a guest appearance on her show – unless she was doing a sequel on hoarding. Throw the brooms out. They are too far gone.

› When Hell Freezes Over

If a daily excursion to the supermarket is not your idea of a pleasure trip, then owning a separate freezer can be a lifesaver. With places like Costco all the rage, freezers have become de rigueur, especially if you like to entertain. Some of our clients are so dependent on them they keep them in living rooms and on balconies if the kitchen, basement or garage is full.

When you have a large enough unit, there is no end to how much food you can cram in them, cram being the operative word. We want to talk about the contents, aka freezer burn casualties.

While a freezer can prolong the freshness of your food, if left in there too long, your groceries undergo a form of decomposition. The tendency is to load the freezer vault to capacity, piling new purchases on top of the old. By the time BBQ season comes around, the raw hamburger patties from last summer look more like the co-stars of a 1950s sci-fi picture. How could you consider eating something resembling a snowball of crystallized maggots? You might be able to use the package of solid frozen peas as an ice pack to ease the swelling from an insect bite. Nevertheless, you would not want to eat them, especially if they came from the freezer bottom. Don't run the risk of a 911 call instead of having dessert.

While you might believe the freezer saves money, it can also drain your financial resources. If buried too deep, you forget you've already bought a box of perogies, so you buy a duplicate. Very organized people avoid this by labeling the date on everything they freeze. If you are reading this book, you are automatically excluded from this upper echelon of the hyper-organized.

We had one client whose freezer was so impacted with food it died. We carried its rotting contents down three flights of stairs and laid it to rest in garbage bins. Believe us, old food is clutter.

» CRUD Challenge

Prepare for your very own in-home polar expedition. You may have to eat your way through it.

Invest in heavy duty large plastic bags. We mean the ones that building contractors use during demolition, not the wimpy bargain knock-off brand from the dollar store. Be ready to responsibly dispose of anything that looks prehistoric, anything you can no longer identify by its weight, shape or coloring and anything resembling a piece of wedding cake from 1981.

You may get lucky and reconnect with the frozen bottle of vodka you forgot you had.

› An Exercise in Futility

What are the three words a woman wants to hear the most? Answer: You've lost weight.

Today's emphasis on health and fitness has generated an enormous market for home exercise equipment. Folks are lured by the promise of flat abs and perky pectorals.

No need to sign up and wait your turn on the sweat-stained treadmill. You have the luxury of 24/7 access to your own private cardio-vascular machine. Unfortunately, few of us actually maintain the commitments we swore to in our New

Year's resolutions.

A few months into making the installment payments, the apparatus falls into disuse. Every time you glance at the idle elliptical machine, you experience feelings of guilt and rebuke. You use it like an auxiliary closet, hanging last season's outerwear from the handlebars. It grows piles of old newspapers and flats of dusty mason jars. Over time you totally camouflage the behemoth. The muffin top you wanted to shed? Just buy a bigger size.

» CRUD Challenge

Not easy. Find a buyer who has the means, motivation and a big house. If selling doesn't work, donate to a school or community center. Remember this frees you up to go to the gym in the company of fellow sufferers.

› Tin Pan Valley

Many delectable treats come packaged in tin containers adorned with reproductions of glistening snow-covered bridges, nostalgic imagery that recollects the simple pleasures of rural life in a century before 10-lane freeways blighted the landscape. Other tins remind us of brands gone by. Whatever the design, these decorative metal vessels garner a huge following. Clients justify their collections in several ways. Sometimes the tired mantra "too good to throw away" is invoked. Inveterate bakers claim them to house the holiday baking they will undertake in December. Some people intend to save them for button collections or loose change.

Maybe you're convinced the tins are collectors' items and will someday fetch a king's ransom on eBay. We aren't. Some of the vintage variety may turn up in a flea market stall or thrift shop. But the blue tins of Danish butter cookies and their ilk are more likely to be stowed away in a disintegrating cardboard box, original crumbs intact, and remain undiscovered until your family moves or the restoration company arrives because the basement flooded.

» CRUD Challenge

Cull your collection and save a choice few, if you must. Consider putting some of the more attractive ones on display. Donate the rest and avoid the paranoia that accompanies throwing away something durable. Do not despair. You are bound to get a few more next season as gifts.

› Butt Out

Once upon a time, smoking was the height of sophistication and a popular pastime symbolically associated with post-coital bliss – not shivering under the eaves in back alleys. In the past, tobacco was king and smokes were plentiful and inexpensive. Table lighters and ashtrays were as common as today's video game controllers.

We remember making ashtrays out of clay in summer camp, using our thumbs to create the little depression for the cigarette to rest. Ashtrays were often coveted gifts coming in a variety of shapes, sizes and designs. Some ashtrays, like the large square glass ones, had enough heft to qualify as lethal weapons and should have been included in the game of Clue, with the candlestick and the wrench.

Because smoking is such an abomination today, ashtrays have disappeared from the home. Yet they do remain, often as collections, in the deep recesses of the basement, dumped into boxes without identifying labels. Ashtrays constitute an example of objects tied to the past whose continued presence defies logical explanation. If you are in possession of such follies, question your motivation. Do you think the irrefutable research documenting the health consequences of smoking will be proven false and that smoking will make a comeback? Even if that were so, could you afford to smoke on your salary?

» CRUD Challenge

If you have perpetuated the myth to your children that you never smoked anything in your youth, the cache of ashtrays might suggest a different story. Carry the whole box out to the curb and label *Take Me* across the top.

CHAPTER 15

PURGATORY

RESCUING YOUR CAR FROM PREMATURE BURIAL IN THE GARAGE

Pity the poor car, left outside year after year to fend for itself against the elements. It bakes in the summer, is drenched by relentless rainstorms and is pummeled by ice and snow in the winter. Your expensive automobile runs the daily risk of some yahoo with a learner's permit plowing into it as he perfects the art of parallel parking. In the meantime, the walls of your garage protect your junk.

Like basements, garages are the ceremonial pitching ground for anything you don't know what to do with. What differs is the nature of the content. Sure, there are plenty of items that make perfect sense to store in the garage. Legitimate use of garage storage includes lawn mowers, gardening tools and supplies, paint, auto parts, bicycles and other sporting goods, patio furniture in the off season and garbage and recycling receptacles.

We don't believe the garage is the ideal location for salting away the ping-pong table that nobody uses, the boxes from every stereo component you ever purchased or the flyers you were supposed to distribute for the community blood drive last year.

› Ho Ho Oh?

Stay focused. What we are about to tell you could be the biggest bang for your buck so far. What do you think are the three most commonly saved items in the home? If you guessed paper and clothing, in the number one and number two positions, then give yourself a pat on the back. If you are at a loss for the third leg of the triangle, look no further than your assortment of holiday decorations. Christmas is the big winner, but Halloween is a strong runner up. Our clients exhibit an almost insatiable hunger for holiday glam. Many have invested small fortunes in the lights, tableware, ornaments, artificial trees, candles, welcome mats, special bakeware and everything else that sparkles or comes in red and green – or orange and black. One downsizing client admitted to owning 43 containers of Christmas decorations she insisted on moving to her new, smaller location, in defiance of our warnings.

Now, if you're not hyper-ventilating, read on. Consider paring down your most treasured items to three or four plastic containers. Let the rest go. We know this hurts.

When it comes to emotional attachment, Christmas decorations take top honors. We recently worked with a client whose Christmas decorations were damaged by a flood in her crawl space. She was unable to open the containers herself because the odors emanating from them reminded her of her childhood and her family. We warn you this can be an emotional minefield, but if you purge and reduce this addiction to a minor vice, you will reap manifold rewards. You will gain enough space in the garage to park a motorcycle or a couple of bicycles, if not a small hybrid car. Then you can use the containers for storing other things more worthy of preservation.

» CRUD Challenge

Not all Christmas decorations are created equal. Some are more deserving of the purge treatment than others. You probably know what they are. Let's begin with outdoor lighting. Since you've upgraded to the more environmentally friendly LED variety, what kind of weird logic is justifying the continued presence of the hairball of multi-colored old style lights?

Count the number of tree stands you own. Tree stands are a little like wine openers. You're always ready to pay for one that works better than the one you have.

Be ready to ditch any ornaments you have not removed from the box in six years.

Holiday lawn ornaments take up more space than they're worth. Those twinkling white deer cannot keep nibbling on your front yard forever. Size matters.

Put plastic poinsettia plants with glitter on the leaves on your endangered species list. Our own favorite candidates for annihilation are last season's fruitcake and singing ornaments activated by motion sensors.

› These Toolish Things

Dirty jobs like small appliance repairs and oil changes, restoring 1960s muscle cars and target practice with a BB gun require a workbench in the garage. Usually these are large rough-hewn boards cobbled together with a vise on one end and a shelf underneath. Someone may have drilled a few holes in yours for the purpose of storing pliers, screwdrivers and a hammer. When you were the prospective buyer of your present home, we bet that workbench was a real selling feature. You imagined yourself stripping and repainting antique furniture or building model trains on lazy Sunday afternoons.

Wake up. Your Fantasy Island has evolved into an Isle of Debris. What's sitting on the work surface – cans and glass jars overflowing with nuts, screws, nails, and washers?

Hockey pads form the base of a pyramid that includes helmets, mitts and golf tees. There is an assortment of sandpaper, beach towels and a garden hose in need of patching.

Speaking of patches, how long has that inflatable boat with the puncture wound and missing oar been waiting for repair?

There's such a jungle in the garage you would not be able to find enough space to super glue a shattered creamer. So if you've surrendered your woodworking dreams and thoughts of do-it-yourself renovation in favor of hiring people, let the workbench remain a catch-all. Otherwise, pitch the excess and whittle down those tools to what you can use.

» CRUD Challenge

This is a rubber glove job – there may be close encounters with rodent droppings. Well, better than coming face to face with the rodent, dead or alive.

In this venture, you will encounter tools often purchased for a specific job or project. Once the job is over, the tools go into retirement. Tools also arrive as Christmas gifts. We think the ideal tool kit should be comprised of an Allen key – to assemble IKEA furniture, a screwdriver for opening china cabinet doors when the original key is lost, and a hammer to move pictures around on your walls. For everything else, you need a telephone.

Collectors sometimes advertise for tools, which are also a big draw at garage sales. If you can't sell, donate to organizations like Habitat for Humanity which re-sell them to raise money for community housing projects.

› Auto Nostalgia

The first exhibit we procured for our Virtual Clutter Museum was a photo of the glove compartment door of a Volkswagen beetle. That was all that remained of our client's beloved coupe, demolished by a Buick.

Many of us find it necessary to hold on to the vestiges of vehicles we drove at various junctures in our past. These questionable artifacts spend years in unheated garages, hidden from view by rusting bicycles and aluminum-framed beach chairs encrusted with mouse poop. These auto remnants include rubber floor mats, the extra seats from the minivan you sold four years ago, children's car seats and two sets of snow tires that won't fit either of the cars you own now.

» CRUD Challenge

Car souvenirs are among the most ignored and neglected of household clutter denizens. Once you've eliminated them, you might have room to park your car, much to the chagrin of local teenage vandals who've taken your Toyota for joy rides on at least five occasions.

› Camping Jeer

Once upon a time, when money was short and the kids were young, summer holidays meant piling into the car à la *Grapes of Wrath* and traveling to a family campground or lakeside retreat. As the years went by you upgraded your holiday requirements to include spa treatments and three-star dining. You concluded that a night ensconced in Egyptian cotton bed sheets makes for a better night's rest than sleeping in a bag atop a roll of backpacker's foam.

Yet, if you venture to the upper shelving unit of your garage, somewhere between the broken sprinkler and the can of brake fluid, you'll find the tents, poles, stoves, tarps, stakes, sleeping bags in multiple weights, foams, dented pots, backpacks and lanterns that at one time provided sustenance and comfort.

Unfortunately, like other unused items left in unheated spaces, they have suffered the ravages of neglect. You could spread them outside on your lawn on some sunny day. Or you could have them cleaned.

» CRUD Challenge

Decide first. Is there a camping trip in your future? You might be able to salvage the hiking boots for an occasional day hike. The rest won't do you much good at your Mexican Riviera timeshare.

› Cool Jerks

While on the subject of outdoor living, turn your attention to the towering mountain of coolers you've collected – the garage equivalent of luggage. You buy new ones because they have wheels, drink holders or advanced drainage technology, but you never toss the old ones. If they are the old-fashioned metal kind, they are rusted shut. If they are made out of plastic, dirt is engrained in the surface. If your coolers are made from styrofoam, shame on you. They were free to begin with. Admit it, you're afraid to open them because of what you imagine could be living inside.

Coolers take up a lot of space, and unless you are constantly entertaining poolside, they get limited use. Why dedicate so much square-footage to empty containers?

» CRUD Challenge

Coolers present ideal opportunities to re-purpose. Evaluate your current inventory for defects. If you come up with too many in decent condition, turn them into storage containers. Think of the attributes. They are rectangular, stack on top of each other and are insulated. Hide presents in them. Store picnic ware or bagfuls of wool. Get creative. They have value, just not as beer fridges.

› Texting: Old Style

Textbooks constituted a sizable chunk of your meager student budget, so it's understandable how you have difficulty parting with such substantial investments.

We will let you in on a little secret. Once the course has been completed, people NEVER look at them again, and for good reasons. Nobody ever takes a textbook on vacation as summer reading. There's the issue of weight and the information is outdated.

What value are they adding to your life today? Remember when you took those courses and had to read those textbooks? Walking on hot coals would have been a small price to pay to alleviate the deadly boredom. Keep that thought as you lug them to the curb for a mercy pickup.

» CRUD Challenge

What to do with these old tomes? If you are still a university student, you are in the best position for unloading. Remove them as supports for your bookshelf planks and sell them back to the college bookstore, assuming the contents are relevant and the professors have not changed the syllabus. Check with Amazon.com as well.

If you're in your middle years, this may not be so easy. Used bookstores take a dim view of these cumbersome volumes. Donation and recycling are your best options. Otherwise use a few to flatten a poster that's been rolled up in a cardboard tube for a decade or two.

› The Dead Pet's Society

Owning pets is a highly satisfactory family experience. You can teach your children about compassion and responsibility. Learning to take care of a pet might even inspire a child to attend veterinary school. But for most of us, problems arise when the adored creature – lizard, Siamese fighting fish, rodent, whatever – passes away. The former habitat – tank, leash, bowl or scratching pole – insinuates itself as a permanent shrine in Snowball's memory. It strikes us as morbid, especially when the family refuses to undergo the trauma of losing a pet a second time, and will never need those cages or chew toys again.

» CRUD Challenge

This one calls for delicacy. Once you've unearthed the dust-covered turtle bowl, plastic fish tank and the hamster wheel, take them out in stealth-mode for donation. We promise that this is the better way.

› Don't Make Me Over

This is a many-headed hydra – the home renovation bug. Almost everyone who lives anywhere succumbs to this, even if it means splashing on a coat of new paint or hanging a shelf. For the dedicated home improvement types, renovation fever borders on obsession, not unlike Phyllis Diller's addiction to plastic surgery. If this describes you or someone you know, the interior of your household might smack of total perfection. The garage, sheds, crawl spaces and backyard proffer a darker image.

That gourmet kitchen, spa-like bathroom or family room expansion takes materials. So what happens to the old particle-board kitchen cabinets? What do you do with old plumbing fixtures? Or the ends of carpet rolls? We find them booted into the garage to wait it out for eternity or until the house gets sold.

Paint persists beyond reason. Everyone keeps at least half a dozen cans of mostly dried up leftover paint in case of a touch up. But we discover shades of lilac or aqua that do not appear on any visible wall. Floor tiles, wood panels, drywall sheets, ceiling tiles, pot lights, broken windows and old doorknobs, cans of stain, toilet seats, faucets and pipes of various lengths line the shelves. The impression is that of a ghostly hardware store.

» CRUD Challenge

First congratulate yourself for not getting divorced. Few marriages can sustain serial renovations.

As you might have guessed, getting rid of construction debris is not a one-person job. It requires padded work gloves and a crew. Schedule an entire day or weekend for this project, depending on the level of debris. Get your recycling bins ready.

For most of the garbage, only heavy duty contractor's garbage bags will handle the weight and pointy ends. If you don't own a truck, make an unbreakable date with a junk remover. If there is a mountain of derelict wreckage, a dumpster may be a good idea.

That was the prep. For doing the deed, employ a little cunning and guile. Since the family members you recruit

" I want to be buried in that dress.
The color really suits me."

CRUD logic from a woman
treasuring a 1960s prom dress.

may be less than enthusiastic about your cleanup project, we suggest the following: Hide all remote controls, smart phones and other communication devices until the work is complete. No incoming calls should distract your worker bees. Make food ahead of time that can be eaten on the fly. That avoids long rest periods for meals. The job will get done quicker. Make a pact with yourself. Hire a contractor for your next renovation, making him responsible for removal – or learn to love your home in its current state.

› Good Sport

If you have extinguished any hope of being drafted by the NHL or being awarded a full athletic scholarship to a Big 10 school, it's time to retool your aspirations to something more attainable, like getting your CPA.

Sports and recreational activities deliver a lifetime of enjoyment, improved fitness and weekly visits to the chiropractor. Participating in sports adds to the quality of life and sports equipment adds to the quantity of life.

Let's start with winter sports. How many pairs of skis, boots and poles are hanging on your walls? Add in the skates, figure and hockey, the sticks, nets and protective gear. Don't forget about the snowboards and cross-country gear. Moving into spring, count up the bats, balls and mitts, along with the two and three-wheeled transporters like bikes and scooters. Basketballs, volleyballs, footballs, soccer balls, tennis balls. You have them by the bucketful. With summer, out come the golf clubs, inflatable pools, rafts and pool toys and possibly a kayak with paddles. If all of this stuff were to disappear, you'd have no trouble parking a tractor in the garage.

Stay with us here. We are not advocating the unloading of your entire collection. Employ a critical eye. For example, if you are scheduled for your second knee replacement surgery, we bet there are no more black diamond runs in your future.

» CRUD Challenge

Divide and conquer. You have many avenues open for sale and distribution.

Start with the kids' stuff. They outgrow their equipment every year or two. Pass on the undersized helmets, elbow protectors, pails and shovels and even uniforms to other parents looking to save money. Try the consignment stores that specialize in sports equipment. Garage sales and swap meets are other good options, as well as donations to schools and community groups.

Take this opportunity to get rid of your older generations of golf and tennis gear. Weed out the rusted, mangled and infirm equipment. Then set your sites on the big game – finding a home, other than yours, for the above-ground pool, trampoline and swing set that occupy the backyard.

CHAPTER 16

PAPER TRAIL
THE ONLY WAY TO FIND YOUR OFFICE

Around the mid-point of the 20th century, futurists predicted a society where leisure time would increase as work diminished, owing to advances in automation. Wrong. In spite of the many labor saving devices introduced over the last 50 years, most people work harder and longer hours than their predecessors. This phenomenon has made the home office de rigueur for many households. Can't meet the day's deadlines at the office? You can continue to work into the wee hours in your home.

But it's not just the unpaid overtime that we perform in our home office refuge. Many companies and employees have opted to telecommute. And there are legions of defectors from the corporate world choosing to open small businesses run out of their home offices.

The home office also functions as an accounting center for home finance, a repository for reading matter and storage for expired catalogs. The home office is where most computers live, making it arguably the room where we spend most of our hours at home. It's where we download our favorite music, watch movies, email, surf the net and connect with old loves from high school on Facebook.

So much goes on in the home office today little things like maintenance are overlooked. People replace obsolete technology without recycling the old. But nothing compares with the tsunami-like tyranny of paper. Bills, receipts, notepads, greeting cards, journals, homework, legal documents and computer printouts top the list. You would doubtless choose a root canal or 2000 sit-ups over sorting through your piles and file cabinets. Our best advice? Be kind to your shredder.

› Yellow Journalism

Magazines are the semi-precious stones of the paper world – not as enduring as books, but more deserving of preservation than the lowly newspaper. We purchase them on newsstands or welcome them into our homes through subscriptions. Once they gain entry, they pile up. You have the best intentions of reading them, but never find the time. Yet the subscriptions keep coming. There is one periodical, above all, that lodges itself permanently (like the plaque on your teeth if you don't make regular visits to the hygienist) – the venerable National Geographic.

You will find these magazines in your office, under the stairs, in the basement or garage, in the far reaches of a guest room closet. It is sacrilege to throw them out. They are preserved even if mildewed. There could be hundreds if not thousands of magazines lounging around in storage space you could dedicate to shoes or Costco purchases.

» CRUD Challenge

Tread carefully. The National Geographic hoarder in your household may be someone other than you. Men, in particular, have a nostalgic affinity for this pre-Internet window into the world. Yes, the photography is second to none, but not justification for holding on to 30 unopened cartons yellowing with age. Hone your negotiating skills. Whittle down the collection to a banker's box or two. Offer to give up a couple of curling irons in exchange.

› Yesterday's Papers

Calendars fall under the rubric of the uninvited. Decorated with splashy illustrations of antique autos, endangered species or exotic tropical destinations, they promote real estate agents and home insurance brokers. Sometimes we purchase them ourselves in bookstores at 70 per cent off, once the mid-point of the year has been reached. People use them to record the minutiae of daily life – dental appointments, social occasions, bottle drives, parent teacher conferences and the like. When posted in a high traffic area in the home, calendars make excellent organizing tools accessible to the entire family.

Unfortunately our clients hold on to them indefinitely, long after their purpose has been achieved. They claim they want to keep them for reference, as if where they had dinner on a night in July of 1992, makes for a gripping reading experience. Does it matter if you have no record of the bridge classes you attended or what day the city picked up your recycling seven years ago? Most people have too many problems meeting the demands of the present to wallow in mundane nostalgia.

» CRUD Challenge

Take a double-pronged approach to calendar infestation. The first line of defense is the front door. Open and review all unsolicited flyers and junk mail over a recycling bin. Save one or two calendars that you find appealing, say the one with wildflowers. When the end of December rolls round, donate the photos of the previous year's calendar to your child's elementary classroom teacher for art projects. Recycle the pages containing your personal notations. Consider ways you can store that information electronically.

› Homeward Bound

Can you recollect shopping for supplies at the start at every school year? The thrill of taking your list up and down the aisles, filling your basket with writing implements, pencil cases, rulers and pristine packages of lined paper? Those shopping sprees heralded the promise of new beginnings, a blank slate of opportunity to reinvent oneself in a new grade with a new teacher. Those were the moments when you began your lifelong love affair with the three-ringed binder, each subject delineated with its own divider and colorful plastic index tab. What an ingenious method to organize schoolwork.

Fast forward another 30 or 40 years to your home office. Observe what's populating your bookshelves that are bending in the middle from excessive weight. We cannot begin to estimate the number of binders we have removed from our clients' offices. We recycle them by the box load.

What makes binders so compelling? Experience tells us that what is filed in a binder is as likely to be retrieved as the lone peanut a squirrel buried in your outdoor plant container last year. In our opinion, binders have persisted into the 21st century because of our basic distrust of electronic media. We hit print for anything we deem worth saving. Binders confirm that hardcopy is still king. Binders present a major roadblock in your quest for an ideal home office.

» CRUD Challenge

This is not a two-second undertaking sandwiched between coloring your hair and waterproofing your new boots. This project will take all the determination you can muster.

- Give away your three-hole puncher. That way you won't compound a situation already out of control.
- Open the first binder and ask yourself: Does it matter what the bank balances were for the Brownies' cookie sales in 1976? Would anyone care if you shredded the council

minutes from the condo you sold 14 years ago?

- What about the condition of those binders? Did you retrieve them from your kid's backpack at the end of the school year? Are they blanketed with iridescent stickers and doodles? Are the spines broken? Is the plastic coating peeling?

- Once emptied of worthless content, reuse some of the binders for photo storage or scrapbooking or to store financial records. If your binders are in good condition, contact a local school or charity for donation. Now you have no more excuses. Grab a snack and get to it.

› Manual Labor

Manufacturers of every domestic appliance, power tool, phone and computing device keep the saw mills humming by inundating us with user manuals and warranty information. Not only do they believe we have engineering degrees, but that we are also linguists, given the number of languages they include. The truth is that the majority of us never look at these, other than to peruse the easy install flyer. Most of this information languishes in bulging accordion files or is crammed into some drawer that refuses to open. Chances are you still have the user guides from the time your cellphone was the size of a shoebox. Or you own illustrated instructions for assembling an entertainment unit long gone.

» CRUD Challenge

Scour your user manual library and at least recycle the ones for the devices you no longer possess. Toss the instructions written in alphabets you are unable to identify.

› Scribblers

How many pens, pencils, and markers have crossed your palm in the course of a lifetime? Pens are seasoned world travelers. A pen may start out on the blotter of a desk in a hotel room only to be whisked away by the road warrior guest who in turn leaves it with a purchasing agent at his first appointment who uses it to initial a new order for ball bearings. It may hang around that office before getting picked up by a co-worker who jots down a phone number and forgets to return the pen to its former keeper. And so it goes. Pens are in a constant state of mobility, alighting occasionally until they hit the ultimate roadblock – your house. Once a pen crosses your threshold it may bounce around among family members, perhaps even exiting by backpack to the local school. The majority end up in the junk drawers of various rooms. The mother lode resides in the desk drawer in your office.

New pens are purchased all the time. Gel pens are a step up from the skinny plastic ballpoints. Within the category of felt markers alone there are many choices of scent, size and permanency. No matter how many pens and pencils you possess at this moment, come September, if you have school-aged children, your stash will double. Now is the time to do something about it or you may find yourself in this predicament:

You are ordering theater tickets by phone. The agent starts to recite the confirmation number. You politely ask the agent to hold while you get a pen. You open the drawer and grab the first one. It's out of ink. Next you reach for a pencil with teeth marks. There is no point. The Sharpie is missing its cap and has dried up. Eventually, you have to rely on committing the 12-digit number to memory. Lotsa luck.

» CRUD Challenge

This takes time and effort, but try to visualize the outcome. Every time you need to write a check, sign a permission slip, capture an address or simply doodle, there will be a choice of pens and pencils in excellent working order.

Dump out the entire cache, and one by one test the pens. The ones that are finished are done. They will not miraculously learn to write again. Hold on to the best of the lot. Donate what makes sense to a non-profit – small charitable organizations rarely have big budgets for office supplies.

› Tourist Traps

Somewhere in the back of your overstuffed file cabinet or stowed away in manila envelopes or plastic bags, lurks the paper residue of countless vacation destinations. The assortment consists of brochures from visits to gawk at the World's Largest Pair of Cross-Country Skis, maps, guidebooks, ticket stubs, advertisements and phone numbers for the cozy cabins you wanted to recommend to friends. The justification for keeping this cache of information is based on the assumption it will not be available at some future date. Not true. The Internet is an invaluable resource of information on any subject, but indispensable for vacation planning. Why resort to a guidebook 10 or 15 years out of date, when you can consult a source filled with current pricing, availability and schedules? Chances are you've not so much as glanced at this useless pile of memorabilia since you returned from that European holiday you took before the kids were born.

» CRUD Challenge

Experts say we do not look at 80 per cent of what we file in cabinets. We are certain that the travel stuff falls in that statistic. Chuck the info so yellowed the print is unreadable. Would life be unbearable without a return visit to Graceland?

› Mystery Keys

Proceed to the nearest desk drawer. Open it. We speculate that among the grimy postage stamps, candy wrappers, bottle caps and staple removers, you will find multiple keys of unfamiliar origin.

To whom or to what do they belong, since they don't fit any of the doors or furniture in your present dwelling? Is that the key entrusted to you by neighbors to keep as a spare? Is that gold one from the apartment you shared before you dropped out of college? Could that odd-shaped key be from the old bicycle lock you threw away last summer? What about the tiny silver ones? They may belong to the suitcase you gave to your son to take to South America. If you dig a little further you may come across one or two mystery locks as well. And what do you know, there's that motel key to room 305 you neglected to drop in a mailbox.

» CRUD Challenge

Wouldn't it be great if your efforts turned up the missing key to your safety deposit box? Then you could access your good jewelry and impress your friends at the wedding you're attending next week. Do not second guess yourself. Chuck the mystery keys once and for all.

› Office Automation

Are you writing checks and doing personal correspondence at the kitchen table because there's no room in your office? This is a complaint we hear all the time from self-employed professionals. The office could offer untold possibilities if only the collection of obsolete office automation products disappeared. If your home office could be mistaken for an electronics recycling depot, get busy.

How much of a geek are you? Did you volunteer to take home that fax machine, large enough to qualify as a helipad, that your company was replacing a dozen years ago? Does your procession of printers encompass everything from the dot matrix to ink jet to laser? How many scanners, routers, modems, external hard drives, extra keyboards, and old laptops are teetering on the top of your desk, credenza, bookshelves and file cabinets?

You get hooked on the thrill of the upgrade without disposing of the previous generation of technology, creating a turf war between paper and electronics. At least bury your old computers and accessories in the basement or garage where they can commiserate with the TVs, stereo components and VCRs. If you decide to unload or repair some of this assemblage, you might be in for a few surprises. Wouldn't it be great to find your missing, presumably dead, cordless phone?

» CRUD Challenge

Good news for technophiles. The options for recycling are expanding. Enterprising companies are springing up that will accept your unwanted machines, re-use the usable parts and dispose of the remains. Many municipalities have added computers to their rosters of recyclable materials. Don't stop there. Ditch the oodles of old disks and CDs. Is one of your desk drawers dedicated to power supplies and obsolete connectors?

Go on line to get help. Start the exodus now.

> **Business Card Blight**

Though small in stature, these humble advertising vehicles manage to evade the fate afforded to unsolicited flyers, and make it to the sanctuary of your desk. Everyone has a business card today, even if unemployed.

This is what happens when you accept a business card: you tuck it into an available pocket and immediately forget about it until you retrieve it from the garment and abandon it on the nearest available surface.

Some business cards are slotted for follow-up, either through phone or email. But if you are like most people, the little cards pile up next to your computer or telephone.

Some people like to keep business cards in small binders that resemble miniature photo albums. Others store them in rolodexes. Even those scanned into computers hang around for no discernable reason. If you happen to have changed jobs, there's a better than even chance that you are harboring half-used boxes of cards denoting your employment history. What

*" I will have to remove all of the
data before I let these go."*

*CRUD logic from a woman storing ancient floppy diskettes
even though her current computer has no floppy drive.*

value could these add to your current life, other than dredging up unpleasant memories of the time you were passed over for promotion or worked in the cubicle sans window?

» CRUD Challenge

Business card organization requires vigilance. Recycling is an ethical and appropriate policy for these cards, like the ones from psychics and tarot card readers. The biggest issue with business cards is there diminutive size. Like little pieces of paper, they can be lost in the uproar or everyday life. If you've been collecting for a while, you are probably overdue for a purge. Here's how to sort them:

- Throw away any card that smacks of multi-level marketing credentials, now reborn as network marketing. These include cards hawking miracle energy drinks and nutritional supplements made from exotic berries that promise eternal youth and relief from diseases you never thought existed.
- Toss cards bearing the names of alternative health practitioners who advocate the curative properties of colonics or leeches.
- Eliminate any business cards that have remained in your possession from the time you had your braces removed in junior high.
- Keep any card that claims "we buy old junk."

> Take this Job and Shove it

Unlike our ancestors, most of us will toil in a series of unrelated careers, until retirement beckons. Yet many of our clients retain stacks of files and folders filled with the detritus of projects from former jobs. When probed as to why, the responses are vague.

When we explain that the possibility of ever needing these or even looking at them is slim to none, we still encounter resistance. Teachers and writers cannot be convinced otherwise. Everything has value for a lesson plan or future book. Keeping these old papers is a way of preserving the former self.

At some point, you need to face the fact that in your current profession as gemologist or exotic dancer, what you did as a customer service representative for the phone company has no relevance. The longer these files gather dust, mildew and silverfish, the more obsolete they become. Recall the reasons you left that job in the first place. Could you ever imagine putting up with that toxic boss, annoying co-workers, pitiful paycheck, soul-destroying commute or merciless workload again? Exorcise those demons by shedding the remaining paper vestiges.

» CRUD Challenge

Think about the big cleanup. Very few of us are required by law to keep work files at home for an indefinite period. Don't transport all this worthless paper out to the garage where it will curl or mildew. Recycle. Or if you think there's sensitive material, shred away.

CRUD SLAYERS

- Never leave home empty handed.

- Follow the one-in one-out rule.

- Never use the "f" word —"for now."

- Avoid the too-good-to-throw-out syndrome.

- Consign early, while items are still in fashion.

- Cherish the memory, not the object.

- Always empty pockets and purses — they are a rich source of CRUD.

- Never decline a charity pickup for donations.

- If you can't sell an item at a garage sale, don't drag it back home.

- Find out when your neighbors are out of town. Double your recycling with their bins.

CHAPTER 17

LIVING END

By this point, you might be asking yourself, "What's next?" If you've managed to eradicate even a portion of what we've identified, you've accomplished a great deal. No doubt you may have discovered more CRUD on your own.

Even if you no longer fear the sound of the doorbell or unexpected visits from relatives, you may have misgivings about the future. Will the CRUD return the moment you relax your guard? No matter how relieved you are to have dispensed with your least treasured possessions and despite your Herculean efforts, understand all you've done is draw a line in the sand. Life will carry on at its relentless pace. New stuff, welcome and otherwise, will arrive daily. Some of it will be yours. The rest will belong to people you know and love. First and foremost, plan a strategy that allows you to make room for new things without having to call in the cavalry. An ounce of prevention is worth a storage locker's annual rent of cure.

BUILD STRONG RESISTANCE

› Don't Try to Make It Look Better

A significant proportion of our clients don't want to give anything away. If your objective in rounding up and booting out the CRUD has been a tactic to replace it with more but different stuff, then you've missed the point entirely. This book is not about hanging more shelves to house bigger collections or installing organizers to double the capacity of your closet. Making everything neat and tidy improves your world – sometimes seeing the floor for the first time in years is an epiphany, but filling every cavity from floor to ceiling will not give you breathing space. If you keep it all and make it look better, what will you do the next time you grocery shop or an appliance breaks? Where will a guest hang up her coat? Will you designate the swimming pool as storage space or buy the house next door to hold your stuff? Will you eat up next semester's college tuition on baskets, see-through bins and labeling tape?

› Don't Make Yourself So Busy

From the standpoint of the professional organizer, being too busy is the devil's workshop for household neglect. Our clients lead extremely busy lives. Many are workaholics who excel at their chosen professions to the exclusion of almost everything else. Others take volunteer and care-giving activities as seriously as they do their work commitments. Many are sports and recreation enthusiasts, take classes or follow artistic and creative pursuits. They are parents cum chauffeurs. They read. They travel. They entertain, belong to clubs and cook. They garden. Life is full and rich. Consequently there is little or no time allotted for cleanup and maintenance of the nest.

If you are truly serious about sustaining your clutter-reduced lifestyle, we implore you to slow down. Quit over-volunteering, over-working, over-parenting. Stop over scheduling yourself and your family, filling every waking moment with a surfeit of endless tasks and activities. Don't over commit. Recognize that everything takes more time than you think. Get off the treadmill.

› Buy for the Right Reasons

By now you should be convinced that you can't have it all, not with the price you pay in disarray. Of course you will continue to shop for the rest of your life. But establish some appropriate ground rules. Avoid the lure of the bargain. If you don't have room, it isn't a bargain. If it's not your size, what's the point? We have supplied countless examples of how impulse and false economy get you in trouble. Was it really worth the pennies you saved on those toilet paper rolls now occupying every cabinet, closet and shelf in your home? If you make purchases in large quantities, especially perishables, will you use or consume them prior to their expiration dates?

› Don't Buy Based on Fear

If you buy something because you are afraid it won't be available at a future date, question why it might be discontinued.

This rationalization goes hand-in-hand with the "just in case" justification for hoarding anything from food to auto parts.

› Don't Buy Out of Boredom

Now that you are no longer filling your days searching for things all over the house, you will have time on your hands. Don't turn to retail therapy for salvation. Fill your free hours with more worthwhile pursuits like hot yoga or spelunking.

› Take Garage Sales and Thrift Shops Off Your List

Decline invitations to home parties where you feel obliged to purchase candles and expensive bakeware. Cancel the cable subscription that includes access to home shopping networks. Avoid pop-up ads on your computer. Shackle yourself to your bed or submit to voluntary house arrest during post-Thanksgiving Black Friday sales events. Don't congratulate yourself on the message on the outlet sales slip declaring how much money you saved by NOT shopping in a department store.

Your new mantra: One in. One out. Make it stick. Nobody expects you to be a saint. Shopping is both a necessary and pleasurable pastime, but change the old rules. Whenever you buy something, if it is a replacement for something you already own, donate, sell, recycle or throw away the old one. Making this a best practice is the strongest defense you have against CRUD recidivism.

> ## Don't Get Sabotaged

One of the biggest problems you may encounter is opposition from your companions. If you have a legacy of failed attempts to clear clutter in the past, the very people who stand to gain the most from your conversion may be your greatest impediment to carrying it through. They are the ones who have tiptoed around your piles, or were tarred with the same brush due to your slovenly ways. Unfortunately, they are loath to forgive and forget easily. They have witnessed versions of cleanouts before and have earned the right to their skepticism. It's not unusual to see husbands and wives undermine each other with sniping and non-cooperation.

You need all the support you can get to stay clean and sober, so to speak. Get your friends and family on board. They may not be the right people to sort and purge with you, but ask them for encouragement. If you have children at home, use the opportunity for life lessons around hygiene, environmental stewardship and respect for boundaries in relationships. In the best scenario, you may get more than you bargained for. Your behavior may inspire others in the household to conquer their clutter demons.

> ## The Floor Does Not Count as a Storage Area

Ding dong the CRUD is gone. Stand back and admire your handiwork. Sure has made a difference, hasn't it? Savor the moment. You have more work to do. Undoubtedly, your activities have caused more than a minimal amount of disruption around your house. Lots of stuff has traded places with other stuff. Two questions come immediately to mind. How are you going to store it and how are you going to find it again?

The floor, the largest surface area in your home, served as the main storage facility. Those days are over. Don't be too hasty to unload furniture like dressers and shelves. They can be re-purposed to hold paraphernalia.

Find better homes than dilapidated cardboard boxes for your precious crystal and bar ware. Install closet organizers. Look upwards for creative solutions to optimize the vertical space in your abode. Invest in clear containers to take the guesswork out of the contents. Label everything, like your life depended on it, because it does. Visibility and accessibility will render search parties irrelevant.

› Just Say No, No, No

The next time some well meaning colleague, friend or relative offers to give you something, say, a hide-a-bed or a blond wood console television, don't go ballistic on him. Let him know politely that you can't accept his act of generosity. You have neither the space nor the inclination to disrupt the equilibrium of your home environment. Avoid other people's cast-offs.

We know exceptions arise, particularly when they involve

family heirlooms or other one-of-a-kind treasures. You must apply stringent criteria whenever you are confronted with one of these decisions, especially if they involve your kids' belongings. You may not have the stamina to take on Operation Overload again. Guard your newly liberated zones fiercely.

› The Laws of Distraction

You may be armed with a new attitude, but it's vital to acknowledge that the old, messy version of you will reassert itself at every opportunity. Learn to pinpoint the exact moment when, where and how your resolve breaks down. Allow us to elucidate.

You are coming home from work, loaded down with packages from the grocery store. The second you place your key in the door, all hell breaks loose. Your cellphone is ringing, your mail is all over the floor and someone starts talking to you. The bathroom is calling your name. The dog is clamoring for a walk. Consider yourself in jeopardy. Distraction is your opponent. How you handle it makes the difference. Be on full alert. Recognize the warning signals. Otherwise, everything will wind up on some catch-all – like the coffee table – "for now." Maintain your focus.

Here is another example that we encounter quite frequently. You begin a chore in one room that leads you into another part of the house, like taking holiday decorations down to the basement. Once there, you are distracted by another action requiring attention. You forget what you were doing and become totally immersed in the new project – combing through a pile of water-damaged magazines, looking for the swimsuit issue. You have no idea why you went to the basement in the first place. Try not to zigzag between tasks or rooms. Finish the first errand before moving on to other pressing jobs.

› Shine the Light

When people are embarrassed by the crowded condition of their homes, they tend to live in darkness. The shades and blinds are perpetually drawn. The windows and doors are shut, allowing neither light nor air to penetrate the premises. They would rather live in a cave-like atmosphere then run the risk of discovery. This also means they never get a good look at the dust that accompanies this depressing tableau.

Now that you've successfully battled with the clutter, subject yourself and remaining stuff to some light therapy. You no longer have a reason to hide from the outside world. From now on, you can see what you have and when tidy threatens to become chaotic, you will know in a flash. Take corrective action immediately.

› Stay Home

We are convinced CRUD is a major driver for the travel and leisure industry. For people who can't stand their surroundings, a trip furnishes the perfect escape from domestic disorder. But running away doesn't solve the problem, does it?

Instead of parking your hard-earned dollars in the pockets of hotel chains and airlines, consider taking a vacation in your own home. We are not suggesting an all-work and no-play scenario, but devoting dedicated time to regular maintenance that will prevent CRUD. If sacrificing a week on a beach seems too much, then pick a weekend or whatever you can manage, to stay on track with your maintenance. Schedule an appointment with yourself rather than leaving it up to chance. Reorganize the kitchen cupboards, read those magazine clippings you've been saving, track down those missing receipts so you can claim a refund. Top off your week by holding a garage sale to accelerate the disposal momentum. Staying home and knocking things off your to-do list can be more refreshing than changing time zones, hauling baggage or waiting in airport security lines.

› Re-Purpose Your Extra Space

A miracle has occurred. Your extra bedroom, basement or garage no longer houses the dreaded boxes, clothing piles and old newspapers. Carpe diem! Convert that vacant territory into a spa, meditation room or workshop. Are you feeling entrepreneurial? Set up a proper home office. Have you been postponing renovations for a decade or so? Now's the time to update your current look. Whatever you decide, do not wait too long. CRUD creeps in wherever it finds an opening. Claim this province as your own. You deserve it.

› After It's Gone

After your CRUD is gone, don't worry about where it went. It's no longer your problem. If it had value, someone else is making better use of it than you. You have the rest of your life to enjoy without the burden of unwanted possessions.

Throw a party. Invite all the people whose invitations you've accepted but never reciprocated because of CRUD. Have the neighbors in for coffee. Schedule meetings at your house. Enjoy your freedom. And never leave home empty handed.

RESOURCE GUIDE

B ased on our experiences with our clients, we know many are stymied when it comes to off-loading surplus household items, clothing and electronics. We also understand that as soon as information is in print it's often obsolete.

The Internet is your best and usually quickest way to find recycling resources or charitable organizations prepared to accept items in your area. Just Google or search for "recycling" or "charitable organizations" in your city or town. You can also try the Yellow Pages, churches, synagogues, community groups and City Hall.

Professional organizers have a wealth of information
at their fingertips. If you are thinking of working
with an organizer here's how to find one:

Canada: Professional Organizers in Canada (POC)
www.organizersincanada.com
US: National Association of Professional Organizers (NAPO)
www.napo.net

These websites provide you with information as well
as a directory of organizers in your community.

Resource Guide

Below is a list of national or international companies
and organizations that will help you recycle:

Donating Used Items

CLOTHING AND SMALL HOUSEHOLD ITEMS

Canadian Diabetes Foundation: www.diabetes.ca

American Diabetes Association: www.diabetes.org

DDA (Vancouver & Richmond, BC Only): www.develop.bc.ca

Big Brothers Big Sisters (Canada): www.bbbsc.ca

Big Brothers Big Sisters (US): www.bbbs.org

Dress for Success: www.dressforsuccess.org

The Salvation Army (Canada): www.salvationarmy.ca

The Salvation Army (United States): www.salvationarmyusa.org

Hospice thrift stores: (Check your local area or community)

MEDICAL EQUIPMENT

American Red Cross: www.redcross.org

Canadian Red Cross: www.redcross.ca

American Medical Resource Foundation: www.amrf.com

ELECTRONICS

ERA (Electronic Recycling Association Canada): www.era.ca

RESOURCE GUIDE

Computer Recycling United States
www.computerrecyclingunitedstates.com

BOOKS

Local libraries and schools
Book bins for charity (bins located on street
corners around your community)
Used book stores

FOOD

Food Banks: www.foodbankscanada.ca
The Global Foodbanking Network: www.foodbanking.org

GENERAL

www.charityvillage.com (Canada only)
This is a Canadian website for the non-profit
sector where you can find organizations in your
local area that accept a myriad of used items.

**We welcome you to visit our Virtual Clutter
Museum and our website at:
www.goodriddance.ca**

ABOUT THE AUTHORS

Susan Borax and Heather Knittel are professional organizers who started their Vancouver-based business Good Riddance Professional Organizing Solutions, Inc. in 2004. They specialize in helping families downsize.

Susan and Heather regularly deliver workshops on the topic of "too much stuff" to corporate audiences, seniors and women's groups.

Along the way they drew from their experiences with clients to create the rollicking, one-act musical review *Cluttermania* in which they perform. The show led the two organizers to expand in print, documenting what they have seen and heard on the job in this self-help volume *Good Riddance: Showing Clutter the Door*. Their intent is to spur the unmotivated into a final confrontation with their clutter demons, or to at least clean out a junk drawer.

"My mother still cannot believe I am helping organize the homes of other people," says Susan. "I tell her it's a simple case of do as I say, not as I do."

Heather, organized since the womb, is a different story. As a child, her favorite garments were underpants embroidered with the days of the week.

ABOUT THE AUTHORS

Their company has been featured in *Chatelaine*, *The Vancouver Sun*, *The Province*, *Good Times Magazine*, *Canadian Health*, *Renovation Magazine and West Coast Homes*. Susan and Heather appear regularly on TV and radio.

Visit their website at:
www.goodriddance.ca

Good Riddance Professional
Organizing Solutions, Inc.